The Rockwool Foundation F

Study Paper No. 63

Does Growing Up in a High Crime Neighborhood Affect Youth Criminal Behavior?

Anna Piil Damm and
Christian Dustmann

Copenhagen 2014

Does Growing Up in a High Crime Neighborhood
Affect Youth Criminal Behavior?

Study Paper No. 63

Published by:
© The Rockwool Foundation Research Unit

Address:
The Rockwool Foundation Research Unit
Soelvgade 10, 2.tv.
DK-1307 Copenhagen K

Telephone	+45 33 34 48 00
Fax	+45 33 34 48 99
E-mail	forskningsenheden@rff.dk
Homepage	www.rff.dk

ISBN 978-87-93119-04-8

ISSN 0908-3979

June 2014

Does Growing Up in a High Crime Neighborhood Affect Youth Criminal Behavior?[*]

Anna Piil Damm[†] and Christian Dustmann[‡]

Abstract: This paper investigates the effect of early exposure to neighborhood crime on subsequent criminal behavior of youth exploiting a unique natural experiment between 1986 and 1998 when refugee immigrants to Denmark were assigned to neighborhoods quasi-randomly. We find strong evidence that the share of young people convicted for crimes, in particular violent crimes, in the neighborhood increases convictions of male assignees later in life. No such effects are found for other measures of neighborhood crime including the rate of committed crimes. Our findings suggest social interaction as a key channel through which neighborhood crime is linked to individual criminal behavior.

Keywords: Neighborhood effects, criminal convictions, social interactions, random allocation

JEL codes: J0, H43

---

[*] This research was carried out in collaboration with the Rockwool Foundation Research Unit. We acknowledge financial support from Grant 24-03-0288 from the Danish Research Agency and the Norface program on migration. We are grateful to three anonymous reviewers, Torben Tranæs, Jerome Adda, David Card, Scott Carrell, Janet Currie, Kevin Lang, Ed Lazear, Magne Mogstad, Uta Schoenberg, Lawrence Katz, and seminar participants at UC Berkeley, UC Davis, the NBER Summer Institute, UCL, the EUI, and Rand Corp. for useful comments and suggestions. Finally, we thank Annika Vatnhamar and Charlotte Duus for research assistance and Britta Kyvsgaard and Bente Bondebjerg for sharing their knowledge about Danish institutions with us. The authors declare that they have no relevant or material financial interests that relate to the research described in this paper.

[†] Department of Economics and Business, Aarhus University, Fuglesangs Allé 4, DK-8210 Aarhus V. Email: apd@asb.dk.

[‡] Department of Economics, University College London, Drayton House, 30 Gordon Street, London, WC1H 0AX. Email: c.dustmann@ucl.ac.uk.

The question of whether lifelong disadvantage is related to the type of neighborhoods individuals are exposed to at a young age is not only of concern to social scientists but is a key question in the public policy debate (see e.g. early work by Brooks-Gunn et al., 1993, or studies using random assignment by Gould, Lavy, and Paserman, 2004 and 2011, and Oreopoulos, 2003). While crime is an outcome of particular interest, most studies in the literature are focused on the effect of *overall* neighborhood characteristics and are not intended to isolate the effect of neighborhood crime from other factors. [1] A few exceptions are early non-experimental work by Case and Katz (1991), which finds a positive relationship between neighborhood crime and criminal behavior of youth, and a recent work by Ludwig and Kling (2007), which finds no evidence for higher violent crime arrest rates for the Moving to Opportunity (MTO) program participants in communities with higher crime rates. Overall, there is no conclusive evidence thus far on how early exposure to neighborhood crime might affect the longer term criminal behavior of individuals.

In this paper we present new evidence on the relationship between early exposure to neighborhood crime, and subsequent criminal behavior of youth. We exploit a unique natural experiment that occurred in Denmark between 1986 and 1998, when refugee immigrants were subjected to quasi-random spatial dispersal across municipalities.[2] Specifically, our analysis focuses on the children of these individuals who underwent this random assignment before the age of 15, and whose crime convictions we observe in each year between the ages of 15 and 21. The possibility to generate complete histories of these individuals based on multiple administrative data sources allows us to provide rare

---

[1] For instance, based on the Moving to Opportunity (MTO) program, Katz, Kling, and Liebman (2001) and Ludwig, Duncan, and Hirschfeld (2001) find that in the early years after reallocation, males in the treatment group had fewer behavioral problems and fewer arrests, while Kling, Ludwig, and Katz (2005) suggest that relocation often reduces arrests for violent crime in the short run but increases arrests for men in the long run. In a final evaluation of the program, Sanbonmatsu et al. (2011) summarize that overall there are no clearly significant effects of assignment to the MTO treatment groups on arrests or delinquent behavior. Other studies that investigate the association between economic conditions and crime rates include Fougère, Kramarz, and Pouget (2009), Grogger (1998), Gould, Weinberg, and Mustard (2002), and Machin and Meghir (2004).

[2] Our analysis is on municipality level (to which we sometimes refer as "neighbourhoods"), as randomisation took place between municipalities. On average, a municipality in Denmark has about 18,800 inhabitants (in 1993), somewhat larger than census tracts (8,000) and more heterogeneous in size. We will provide robustness checks by excluding the largest municipalities.

2

evidence on the effect of early childhood environment on later crime behavior, based on a research design that addresses the problem of endogenous neighborhood selection.

One important reason for neighbourhood crime affecting the criminal behaviour of youth is social interaction between individuals, which is the mechanism we aim to isolate in this paper. Manski (1993, 2000) distinguishes between two types of social interaction: endogenous interaction, where the propensity of an individual to engage in crime varies with the criminal behaviour of her peer group,[3] and contextual interaction, where the propensity of an individual to to engage in crime varies with the "exogenous" or "contextual" characteristics of residents, such as their economic and social status or their attitudes towards crime.[4] Another reason may be that individuals in the same municipality share the same institutional environments, such as the quality of educational institutions or crime prevention mechanisms, which in turn affect criminal behaviour. These "correlated" effects (Manski, 1993) are not social effects, and they are not created by social interactions. We can distinguish more forcefully than previous work between social effects, induced by social interaction, and correlated effects, through other municipality characteristics affecting delinquent behavior of youth, as the large number of allocation municipalities allows us to condition on a wide variety of municipality characteristics. Moreover, the fact that individuals were assigned to different municipalities over more than a decade provides us with the rare opportunity to control for municipality fixed effects to eliminate all time-invariant municipality characteristics.

One of our key departures from the literature is that thanks to the detailed administrative data, we are able to construct more precise measures of the criminal environment that might affect young people's behavior than used in previous work. In particular, we posit that rates of committed crimes in a neighborhood, a commonly used

---

[3] Endogenous interactions could for instance be mediated through exchange of information among criminals (see e.g. Cook and Goss, 1996, and Becker and Murphy, 2000), social norms, or reduction of social stigma associated with crime as the number of peers involved in criminal activity rises (see e.g. Kemper, 1968). Contact to criminals may further provide information about the present values of particular actions, as in informational role models (see Chung, 2000), or create conformity behaviour, as in moral role models. Manski (2000) distinguishes between three channels for endogenous effects: constraints, expectations, and preferences. He emphasises that even if it was possible to find evidence for endogenous interactions, it will usually not be possible to identify the distinct endogenous channel through which group behaviour affects individual behaviour.

[4] While both endogenous and contextual effects are social effects and are induced by social interaction, only endogenous effects create social multipliers (see Glaeser, Sacerdote and Scheinkman, 1996; 2003).

measure in the neighborhood literature, may not fully capture the criminal context that leads to criminal behavior. If, for instance, young people's criminal behavior is affected by social interactions with other criminal youth, the *share of criminals* in the neighborhood rather than the *rate of committed crimes*, might account for such effect more precisely.

We indeed find strong and systematic evidence that the share of convicted criminals living in the assignment neighborhood at assignment, and particularly the share of those convicted for violent crimes, affects later crime convictions of males, but not of females, who were assigned to these neighborhoods as children. Specifically, we find that a one standard deviation increase in the share of youth criminals living in the assignment neighborhood, and who committed a crime in the assignment year, increases the probability of a conviction for male assignees by between 5% and 9% later in life (when they are between 15 and 21 years old). We do not find any such evidence when we use other measures of crime, such as the rate of committed crimes or adult crime conviction rates.[5]

Our results are robust to conditioning on a large set of neighborhood characteristics, including neighborhood fixed effects. It is primarily conviction rates for violent crime that trigger later criminal behavior and that induce not only violent criminal behavior but also convictions for property crime and drug crime. Most particularly, it is the share of young (<26 vs. >25) criminals living in the area that affects a young man's convictions later in life, and it is criminals from an individual's own ethnic group that matter most. Our evidence also tentatively suggests that young men are the most vulnerable to the effect of delinquent neighborhood influences in their early teens, when they are particularly receptive to role models and peer behavior (see e.g., Ingoldsby and Shaw 2002).

---

[5] That youth criminal behavior responds to the presence of other criminals is also consistent with findings in previous studies that establish clear effects of delinquent peers on one's own outcomes in more confined environments. See e.g. Bayer, Hjalmarsson, and Pozen (2009) who analyze the influence of juvenile offenders serving time in the same correctional facility on each other's subsequent criminal behavior, Carrell and Hoekstra (2010) who find that children from troubled families decrease their peers' test score outcomes and increase misbehavior, and Deming (2011) who shows that peer effects are one explanation for a gain in school quality leading to a significant reduction in crime. Similarly, Sacerdote (2001), using random assignment of Dartmouth College first-year roommates and dorm-mates, identifies peer effects on joining social groups, and Kremer and Levy (2008) report that being assigned to a roommate who drank prior to college has a sizeable effect on males' academic performance.

I. BACKGROUND, DATA, AND EMPIRICAL FRAMEWORK

A. The Danish Spatial Dispersal Policy

In 1986, the Danish Government, through the Danish Refugee Council, implemented a two-stage dispersal policy for asylum seekers whose applications had been approved (hereafter, refugees) with the primary objective of dispersing them across counties and municipalities based on the number of existing inhabitants.[6] Hence, the council first allocated refugees to counties proportional to the number of county inhabitants and then to municipalities within the counties proportional to the number of municipal inhabitants (Danish Refugee Council, CIU 1996, pp. 8–9).[7] Over the 13 years (1986–1998) during which the policy was in force, 76,673 individuals were granted refugee status (*Statistical Yearbook 1992, 1997, 2000*) and allocated across municipalities.[8]

Before being approved for refugee status, asylum seekers lived in Red Cross reception centers across Denmark, but within 10 days of receiving approval, the council assigned them temporary housing in one of Denmark's 15 counties (Danish Refugee Council, CIU 1996, p. 9). After assignment to a county, the council's local office then assigned them to one of the municipalities within the county and helped them find permanent housing.[9] To assist the council with its allocation decision, on receiving asylum, refugees filled in a questionnaire that asked for personal details like birth date, marital status, number of children, nationality - information that could have been used in allocation decisions. Thus, assignment was random conditional on these characteristics, which our analysis includes. By contrast, the council's housing decision was not influenced by educational attainment, criminal record, or family income, as this information was not available to the council. Furthermore, and importantly, there were no

---

[6] Following the usual convention, we use the term "asylum seeker" for a person seeking asylum and the term "refugee" for a person whose asylum status has been approved.

[7] In the policy period, Denmark was divided at the regional level into 15 counties, and at the local level into 275 municipalities.

[8] Edin, Fredriksson and Åslund (2003) use a Swedish assignment policy similar to that studied here.

[9] According to the Danish Refugee Council's 1986–1996 annual reports and 1992–1997 internal administrative statistics, only 0–4% of refugees failed to find permanent housing within the introductory 18-month period.

face-to-face meetings between placement officers and refugees, and the only information available to the placement was that from the questionnaire.

Further, the council did not consider individual location wishes in the assignment process. Moreover, any reassignment request was considered *after* the individuals had first moved to the originally assigned municipality.[10] These points are important for our design because it is based on the randomness of the *first* assignment area and all variables refer to that initial municipality. Once settled in the municipality of assignment, the refugees received social assistance for an introductory 18-month period while participating in Danish language courses. Nevertheless, although the refugees were urged to stay in the assigned municipality during the entire introductory period, there were no relocation restrictions.[11]

This allocation policy was considered a success: according to the council's annual report for 1987, only two years after the introduction of the policy, refugees were living in 243 out of 275 municipalities (Danish Refugee Council 1987, pp. 30–31), and their geographical distribution closely resembled that of the overall population.[12]

Given the way in which the dispersal policy was implemented, the allocation of families across municipalities should not have been responsive to youth crime or correlated with youth crime rates conditional on the information available from the questionnaire, and that the council might have used for allocation purposes (e.g., household size). To test this assumption, we first define six measures of area crime in the municipality of assignment in the year of assignment: youth crime conviction rate, youth violent crime conviction rate, overall crime conviction rate, violent crime conviction rate for the entire population, number of reported crimes per capita, and number of reported violent crimes per 10,000 inhabitants (see Section I, subsection C, for a detailed explanation). We then regress these six measures on the individual characteristics of the

---

[10] Interview on June 8, 2001, with former placement officers Bente Bondebjerg and Morten Iversen. When interviewed again on March 7, 2008, Bondebjerg, by then the Danish Refugee Council's chief consultant, did not recall that any refugee rejected the council's offer of housing assistance.

[11] Table A1 in the appendix reports the survival probabilities for the sample of refugee children we use for our analysis. After eight years, one in two households still lives in the assignment area.

[12] Figures A1a and A1b in the appendix, which outline the settlement of refugee immigrants in Demark in the 1980–1984 (pre-policy) and 1986–1998 (post-policy) periods, clearly show a strong concentration of refugees in the metropolitan areas of Copenhagen, Aarhus, Aalborg, and Odense in the pre-policy period but a fairly even distribution across areas in the post-policy period.

household heads observed by us and by the council at assignment (age, number of children, marital status), and on educational attainment, which is not available to the council but is available to us, conditioned on year of assignment and country of origin fixed effects. We perform these balancing tests for the final sample that we use for the analysis below.[13]

We report the results in Table 1, unconditional (upper panel) and conditional (lower panel) on municipality fixed effects. We include the latter to validate the quasi-randomness of within-municipality variation in time of arrival, as we also estimate models that condition on municipality fixed effects. The F-test on the joint insignificance of the education variables (which are unobserved by the authorities) is not rejected in each case. The number of children (which was known to the council from the questionnaire) is significant in five of the twelve regressions, the likely reason being that it was easier to find housing for larger families in rural areas, where crime rates are lower (see Table A3 in the appendix for the correlations). We also estimate these same regressions for other area characteristics: poverty rate, immigrant share, log of inhabitants, teacher hours per pupil, crime detection rate, and number of police officers per 1000 inhabitants. Again, the educational variables are never statistically significant, with p-values for joint insignificance between 0.12 and 0.95. Finally, we compute the same regressions as in Table 1 on the level of the individual child (instead of the household level). In none of the 12 regressions could the null hypothesis of joint insignificance of the education variables be rejected, with p-values between 0.17 and 0.83 (see Table A2.b in the appendix). Thus, based on these tests, and the way the policy was implemented, we believe that the allocation of refugees to municipalities was quasi-random, conditional on the characteristics known to the council at assignment.[14]

---

[13] We have also performed these tests for the overall sample, including household heads of children whom we do not observe in each year, and therefore exclude from our analysis (see footnote 19, and Table A2.a in the appendix). Results are very similar than those for the estimation sample, which we report here.

[14] We also regressed the youth crime conviction rate in the initial settlement area on the same set of variables for pre-reform refugee fathers (who immigrated 1981-1984), as in column 1 of Table 1. In spite of the low number of observations (N=164), the F-test on joint insignificance of educational attainment dummies cannot be rejected at the 10 percent level, with a p-value of 0.0642.

B. Criminal Justice and Youth Crime in Denmark

Denmark, unlike many other countries, has no juvenile justice system: the minimum age of criminal responsibility is 15 years, above which young people are sentenced in the same courts as adult offenders and in accordance with the same criminal code.[15] For offenders below the age of 18, however, a number of sentencing options are available that do not exist for offenders 18 and older; for instance, the conditions for withdrawing a charge are more lenient, the most frequent sentence for those convicted is a monetary fine, and even when prison sentences are given, they are often suspended.

In our analysis we measure individual criminal activity based on charges and convictions[16] for offenses against the criminal code, which are recorded from the age of 15 onward. We define convictions as court rulings that the suspect is guilty of the charge, signaled by the awarding of a sentence (either a fine, conditional withdrawal of charge, or a suspended or unsuspended prison sentence). A suspect is considered "not guilty" if a "not guilty" verdict was recorded or the indictment was dropped (Statistics Denmark 2005, p. 39). Although charges are typically a predecessor to a conviction, in the sample of refugee children we use for analysis only 29% of charges (excluding Traffic Offenses) led to a conviction. This is similar to the ratio of convictions to charges for Danes: for a random 10% sample of Danes born in 1980 and whom we follow until age 21, we find that 28% of charges led to a conviction.

In the Central Police Register charges and convictions are categorized into eight different types of offenses: sexual assault, violent crime, crimes against property, other offenses against the penal code, offenses against the Traffic Act, offenses against the Drugs Act, offenses against the Arms Act, and offenses against the Tax Acts or other special acts. Individuals convicted for violation of the penal code (e.g., sexual assault,

---

[15] We draw here on an excellent overview of the youth crime justice system in Denmark by Britta Kyvsgaard (2003).

[16] Criminal behavior in the U.S. is most commonly measured by arrests, which in Denmark are not as common. According to the Danish "Law on Administration of Justice" (Retsplejeloven. Article 755, part 1), the police can arrest a person whom they have reason to suspect guilty of a criminal offence subject to public prosecution, but only if an arrest is regarded as necessary in order to prevent further criminal offenses, ensure the subject's presence for the time being or to prevent his communication with other people. Further, an arrest should not be made if imprisonment would be a disproportionate measure in regard of the nature of the offence or other circumstances. As a consequence, and according to Statistics Denmark 2005 (Table 6.04), there were only 42,137 arrests in Denmark in 2005, meaning that only 36% of charges were accompanied by an arrest.

violent crime, crimes against property) or the Drugs Act have a criminal record for 2–5 years after conviction or release from prison depending on the sentence.[17] Throughout the analysis, we omit offenses against the Traffic Act and combine the remaining offenses into four categories: property crimes, violent crimes (including sexual assault), drug crimes, and other offenses (see Table A4 in the appendix, for a more detailed explanation). For these categories, we consider all offenses committed between the ages of 15 and 21 but distinguish between those at ages 15–17 and those at ages 18–21.

C. Data

Primary data sources and samples. We derive our data from three primary sources: the Central Police Register, which records individual crime charge and conviction records for the full Danish population (including refugees); the Administrative Registers, which provide individual demographic characteristics (age, current residence, parents' ID numbers, country of origin, immigrant status, and date of immigration), and the Educational Institution Register and Surveys, which contain data on educational attainment. Because all such information is available for the 1980–2006 period, we can link individual records from the three registers via a unique ID number (the detailed definitions and primary data sources for each variable are given in Table A5 in the appendix).

The information on crime charges includes the date of the charge and the start date of committing the offense. The information on crime convictions includes the date of conviction, verdict, sentence, and type of offense, which can all be linked to the start date of committing the offense. To construct a data set containing different measures of neighborhood crime in each calendar year between 1980 and 2006 for all municipalities in Denmark, we link individual records from the Central Police Register with the Administrative Registers.

Based on the population of all those individuals who have been approved for refugee status, we construct our sample by linking individual records from all three registers and extract observations for refugee children who arrived in Denmark together

---

[17] In our data, we observe all charges and convictions even after the criminal record has been deleted from the individual's file.

with at least one parent between 1986 and 1998 from one of the following eight source countries: Lebanon, Iran, Iraq, Somalia, Sri Lanka, Vietnam, Afghanistan, and Ethiopia.[18] Refugees from these countries accounted for more than 86% of the total number of permanent residence permits granted to refugees between 1985 and 1997. We define a refugee as an individual who (i) immigrated from one of these eight countries during the 1986–1998 period and (ii) at the time of immigration (i.e., the year of receiving a residence permit) was not married to either an individual from a non-refugee sending country or an immigrant from a refugee-sending country who had immigrated at least one year earlier. We impose the latter criterion in order to limit the refugee sample to refugees assigned to a location by the council after being granted asylum.

The children analyzed are the subgroup of refugees who were under 15 at the time of assignment, have at least one refugee parent residing in Denmark, immigrated at most one year after the refugee parent(s), and have records in the registers until the age of 21. We exclude refugee children who cannot be followed up to age 21 in the administrative registers, which comprises 21% of all individuals.[19] The final outcome is a sample of 4,425 children, 55% of them male, whose individual and family background characteristics and country of origin are reported in Table A7 in the appendix. For this sample of children, we observe all criminal convictions and charges between the ages of 15 and 21.

Criminal offences, crime measures, and neighborhood characteristics: The numbers in Table 2 show that 38% of all refugees who arrived in Denmark as children had been charged (first row) and 31% convicted (second row) at least once for a criminal offense by the age of 21. This compares to about 13% (and 11%) for a 10% random sample of Danes born in 1980. Interestingly, the charge rates for males (55%) and

---

[18] Refugees from the former Yugoslavia are excluded from our sample because in contrast to refugees from other refugee-sending countries, they were initially granted provisional asylum and therefore subject to a special refugee dispersal policy implemented in 1993 (the so-called Bosnian program).

[19] Of the 5,615 refugee children who arrived in Denmark before age 15 together with at least one parent, we exclude 975 refugee children who had left Denmark before age 21 and 215 refugee children who were not observed in every year between arrival and age 21. To check whether this attrition is random with respect to our outcome variables, we regress the indicator variable for whether the individual leaves the sample on the youth crime conviction rate in the municipality of assignment, as well as on observed background characteristics. This regression yields a *t*-value for the crime variable of 0.25. If our regressor is the overall crime conviction rate in the municipality of assignment or the youth violent crime conviction rate, the *t*-value is 0.69 or 0.7, respectively (see Table A6 in the appendix).

females (17%) are not dissimilar to the arrest rates reported by Kling, Ludwig, and Katz (2005) for the MTO sample, in which 53% of males and 19% of females had been arrested at least once.[20] Criminal convictions by the age of 21 are also much higher for males than for females, 46% versus 13%. Subdividing convictions by crime type further reveals that, perhaps not surprisingly, the largest contributor is property crime, followed by violent crime.[21]

Panel B of Table 2 shows the distribution of the number of convictions. The number of repeat offenders is considerable: Among men, 60% of those who were convicted at least once, had more than one conviction, and 23% had more than 4 convictions. In panels C and D of the Table, we break down overall charge and conviction probabilities by age ranges 15–17 and 18–21. These figures show for males that 31% and 34% had been convicted for a crime committed in age range 15-17 and 18-21, respectively. As shown in Table A8 in the appendix, where we break down the number of convictions for the two age ranges, about 20% carry convictions for crimes committed in both age ranges. The overlap for females, in contrast, is far smaller.

Our main measure of area youth criminality is the share of individuals aged 15-25 convicted of a crime committed in calendar year t (which we relate to the year of our sample individuals' assignment) and who lived in municipality r at that time. We refer to this share as the *youth crime conviction rate* of municipality r in year t. We further distinguish between the shares of individuals convicted for particular crimes, like violent crimes and property crimes, and compute crime measures for different age ranges. As alternative crime measures, we also compute more commonly used measures of neighborhood crime, such as the number of reported crimes per capita and the number of reported violent crimes per 10,000 inhabitants for each municipality in each year.

We include two sets of municipality characteristics, the first of which comprises the log of the number of inhabitants, the relative poverty rate, the share of immigrants in the neighborhood, the weekly number of teacher hours per pupil, and the pupils per

---

[20] These arrest rates, based on MTO youth aged 15–21 at the end of 2001, capture criminal behavior for that group through the end of that year.
[21] Subdividing property crime further shows that of those convicted at least once for a property crime, 61% of males and 87% of females are convicted for theft. Males also have convictions for burglary (22%), fraud (11%), handling of stolen goods (13%), robbery (17%), and vandalism (10%), whereas the only other large categories for females are fraud (11%) and forgery (6%).

teacher ratio. Glaeser and Sacerdote (1999) hypothesize that the area's "population size" is likely to be related to criminal activity, as well as to opportunity, because it may directly impact returns to crime and arrest probabilities (see also Glaeser, Sacerdote and Scheinkman, 1996). We include poverty as it may be a good summary measure for neighborhood quality (see Kling, Liebman, and Katz, 2007).[22] We include the share of immigrants living in the area because it may relate to neighborhood segregation, thereby inducing social conflict as well as criminal behavior (e.g., Logan and Messner, 1987). We also include the weekly number of teacher hours per pupil in the municipality and the pupils per teacher ratio, to capture school resources that may affect the relative attractiveness of pro- versus antisocial behavior (Sanbonmatsu et al., 2011).[23]

Our second set, constructed to reflect the efficiency and presence of police services in the area, contains two measures of policing. The first is the number of police officers per 1,000 inhabitants in the municipality, and the second, the crime detection rate in the municipality, obtained from administrative police statistics and computed as the number of charges relative to the number of reported crimes (see Table A5.B in the appendix for further details). The allocation of more police resources to areas with higher crime rates may create a correlation between area crime rates and individual criminal convictions. For example, Kling, Ludwig, and Katz (2005) suggest that better policing may increase arrest probabilities, but also deter criminal behavior. Levitt (1997) finds that the size of the police force reduces both violent and property crime (see also Levitt, 1998). We display the correlations between the various crime measures and municipality characteristics across all Danish municipalities during 1986–1998 in Table A3.[24]

---

[22] We compute the poverty rate as the share of adults in the municipality who live in a household that meets the OECD definition of "relatively poor" (i.e., disposable household income below 50% of the national equivalence-scaled median disposable household income).

[23] Lochner and Moretti (2004) find that schooling significantly reduces the probability of incarceration and arrest, and Deming (2011) provides strong evidence that better schools lead to a reduction in crime later on.

[24] Note that all municipality variables are measured in the year of assignment, so that they cannot be affected by assignees' criminal behaviour. However, they are identified in regressions conditioning on fixed municipality effects, as we observe multiple cohorts being assigned to the same municipalities.

II. EMPIRICAL METHODOLOGY AND INTERPRETATION

The main question posed in this paper is whether children assigned to a neighborhood with a higher crime rate are more likely to engage in criminal behavior later in life. Our basic specification represents the criminal behavior of individual i assigned to neighborhood r in assignment year t:

$$(1) \quad y_{itr} = a_1 + a_2{}^{M} G_i C_{itr} + a_2{}^{F} (1 - G_i) C_{itr} + a_3 G_i + \mathbf{X}_{it}\mathbf{a} + \mathbf{T}_t + \varepsilon_{itr}$$

where the variable y_{itr} is an indicator that takes the value 1 if individual i assigned to location r in year t is convicted of a crime committed in the age range 15–21, 15–17, or 18–21. Alternatively, we use the number of convictions. The key variable in (2) is C_{itr}, which we compute as the share of individuals aged 15-25 who were convicted for a crime committed in year t *and who lived in municipality r* to which individual i was assigned in that year (the *youth crime conviction rate*). We compare and contrast this variable to alternative and more commonly used measures of crime, such as reported crime rates. To ease interpretation across specifications, we normalize all crime measures by their standard deviations across all assignment areas and assignment years. To account for differences between individuals' pre-assignment characteristics, including those known to the council at assignment (i.e., household size, country of origin, parental age and marital status) and those not known to the council (e.g., parental educational attainment),[25] the vector $\mathbf{X}_{it}$ contains individual background characteristics in the year of assignment, as well as age at assignment dummies.[26] Further, the vector $\mathbf{T}_t$ contains year of assignment dummies, and ε_{itr} is an error term. To enhance efficiency, we estimate Equation (1) for the pooled sample of males and females but allow both the level and the impact of area crime to differ between genders by measuring the interaction between a gender dummy ($G = 1$ for males) and area crime rates.

---

[25] These variables also account for the variation in socioeconomic background that may be associated with child neglect. For instance, Currie and Tekin (2012) demonstrate a strong association between child maltreatment and future crime.

[26] Notice that age at assignment is perfectly correlated with potential years of exposure, which equals age at observation – age at assignment.

13

In our research design, the quasi-randomization of refugees to neighborhoods ensures that C_{itr} is not correlated with ε_{itr} in (1), conditional on the vector $\mathbf{X}_{it}$ variables that were known to the council when assigning individual families. Hence, the key parameter of interest is $a_2^{\,j}, (j = M, F)$, which, given our research design, is a causal parameter. However, it may not measure the effect that area crime itself has on criminal activity, but rather represent the effect of area crime through its correlation with municipality characteristics, which in turn affect criminal behavior. In our case, the large number of assignment neighborhoods with varying characteristics provides sufficient variation to allow identification of both the effects of neighborhood crime and all plausibly relevant neighborhood characteristics. A further unique characteristic of our experiment is its prolonged implementation over multiple cohorts of assigned refugees, which allows us to estimate the effects of neighborhood crime – identified by differences in crime rates upon assignment across cohorts within neighborhoods – by conditioning on neighborhood fixed effects. Thus, to isolate the effect of crime from other neighborhood and institutional characteristics at assignment, we add a vector $\mathbf{A}_{tr}$ that includes the two sets of municipality of assignment characteristics (whose values refer to the year of assignment) discussed in Section I, subsection C, and we condition on municipality of assignment fixed effects $\mathbf{R}_r$ to obtain:

$$(2) \quad y_{itr} = b_1 + b_2^{\,M} G_i\, C_{itr} + b_2^{\,F} (1 - G_i)C_{itr} + b_3 G_i + \mathbf{X}_{it}\mathbf{b} + \mathbf{A}_{tr}\mathbf{d} + \mathbf{T}_t + \mathbf{R}_r + e_{itr},$$

where e_{itr} is an error term.

III. Results

A. Main Estimation Results

Effect of youth crime conviction rate on criminal behavior. Table 3 reports our estimates for the coefficients on the neighborhood youth crime conviction rate at assignment, normalized by the standard deviation, for males (panel A) and females (panel B). Specification (1) conditions only on a gender dummy. Specification (2) also conditions on year of assignment fixed effects, country of origin fixed effects, age at assignment dummies, family background characteristics (one dummy each for single parent, number of siblings, and father and mother's educational attainment and age), and the log number

14

of individuals from the same origin country in Denmark, all measured at the time of assignment. Specification (3) additionally includes area characteristics that measure the neighborhood's socioeconomic context (log of inhabitants, poverty rate, share of immigrants, the weekly number of teacher wage hours per pupil, and the pupils per teacher ratio). Specification (4) additionally conditions on the crime detection rate and number of police officers per 1,000 inhabitants as measures of police efficiency and presence. Finally, Specification (5) additionally conditions on municipality fixed effects. The standard errors take into account the clustering of the observations by municipality of assignment.

In the first block of each panel, we report the coefficients of the youth crime conviction rate in the assignment year in the assignment municipality when the dependent variable is a binary indicator for at least one conviction in the 15–21 (first row), 15–17 (row 2), or 18–21 (row 3) age range; in the second block, we report results when the dependent variable is the number of convictions. Results refer to our sample of youth assigned to an area before age 15, with the average age at assignment being 9. Convictions for crimes committed at age 15 or later are, on average, convictions for crimes committed at least six years post assignment.

The results for males, given in panel A, Table 3, point to a positive effect of the share of convicted youth criminals in the area of first assignment at assignment date on the probability of later conviction. Unconditional on background and neighborhood characteristics, the probability of later conviction in the 15–21 age range is about 2 percentage points higher in an area with a one standard deviation higher area youth crime conviction rate. The estimate is similar for convictions in the other two age ranges (18–21 and 15–17). Conditioning on background and neighborhood characteristics (see columns (2-4)) changes the coefficient estimates only slightly. Overall, the point estimates for the 18–21 age range are slightly more precise and larger than those for the 15–17 age range. The estimates in the second block of panel A, in which the number of convictions is a dependent variable, are larger, and estimates remain similar across specifications.

Column (5) reports the results of additionally conditioning on all area characteristics that are fixed over time; for instance, neighborhood-specific "cultures" of attitudes toward crime that affect policing or reporting, or differences in institutions or social composition that are not captured by our neighborhood variables but are correlated with crime rates and individual convictions alike. For conviction probabilities, the estimates for crimes committed in the 18–21 age range increase only slightly, while those for the 15–17 and 15–21 age ranges nearly double in magnitude.[27] A similar pattern emerges for the estimates on number of convictions. Overall, these findings provide solid evidence that the share of youth convicted for a crime committed in the assignment neighborhood during the assignment year leads to an increase in crime convictions of children assigned to that neighborhood in that year. Based on the estimates in the last two columns, and given the overall conviction rate (number of convictions) of 46% (1.48 convictions) for male refugee youths aged 15 to 21, a one standard deviation higher youth crime rate in the assignment area increases the probability of a crime conviction by between 5% and 9% and the number of convictions by between 7% and 11%. Translating our estimated effects into percentage effects, our estimates in the two last columns show that a one percentage point increase in the youth crime conviction rate in the assignment area increases the probability of a crime conviction by between 7% and 13% and the number of convictions by between 10% and 16%. With few exceptions, other neighborhood characteristics have no effect on criminal behavior (see Tables A9.A and A9.B in the appendix, where we report estimates for the effect of neighborhood characteristics, conditional and unconditional on the youth crime conviction rate).[28]

For females, as shown in panel B, the estimates are much smaller and in none of the specifications are they statistically significant, findings that stand in contrast to those for males. These estimates do not point to any systematic relation between area youth crime conviction rates at assignment and individual criminal behavior. They are in line with the criminology literature that suggests males and females react differently to detrimental neighborhood conditions.[29] These findings are also in line with an increasing

---

[27] This suggests that municipality fixed effects capture some unobserved area components that are positively correlated with the share of criminals in the area, but reduce individual propensities to commit crime. One such factor may be crime preventive measures for children and youth at the municipal level that have initially been implemented in high crime municipalities, as a cooperation between schools, social services department and police (SSP-cooperation) (www.dkr.dk/ssp-samarbejde).

[28] We also run regressions using Specifications (4) and (5) in Table 3 in which we additionally condition on all the interaction terms of the youth crime conviction rate and the neighborhood characteristics. All these interaction terms are insignificant.

[29] For example, Clampet-Lundquist, Edin, Kling, and Duncan (2011) conclude, based on interviews with youth from the MTO experiment, that male youth have more negative peer exposure because they spend

16

number of experimentally based studies that point to gender differences in response to social context.[30] Our findings for any of the following estimations indicate no systematic relations between female criminal behavior and neighborhood characteristics, so for the remainder of the discussion, we focus on the results for males only.

Robustness checks. In Table 4, we report the results of various robustness checks in which we use specifications that correspond to Specifications (4) and (5) in Table 3 and focus on crimes committed in the 15–21 age range. In panel A, we report the results from Table 3 (males) as a reference; in panel B, we use criminal charges, rather than convictions, as an alternative measure for individuals' criminal behavior. These specifications produce estimates with larger standard errors, in particular for the number of charges, suggesting that crime charges are a noisy measure for criminal propensity (only 29% of charges lead to convictions, see Table 2). This supports our use of crime convictions as a measure of criminal behavior.

Our measure of neighborhood is municipalities, which is the spatial unit across which random assignment took place, with about 18,500 inhabitants on average. One concern may be that this neighborhood definition is too large and could result in less precise estimates. On the other hand, defining neighborhoods too narrowly may lead to the omission of a considerable number of interactions. We investigate these concerns computing the residency of co-offenders for the first crime for which individuals have been convicted.[31] About one in four first convictions was for a crime for which at least one other offender was convicted. Of these co-offenders, 34% lived in the same smaller spatial area in the year of committing the crime (with an average of 2,300 inhabitants),

---

their free time in closer proximity to illegal activity than do females. As also pointed out by Steffensmeier and Allan (1996), crime is stigmatizing for females and thus has a greater potential cost to life chances. Mears, Ploeger, and Warr (1998) suggest that, given the same choices, males are more likely than females to have delinquent friends, and negative peer influence is reduced or even counteracted by females because of stronger negative moral evaluations.

[30] For instance, Kremer and Levy (2008) find that previous alcohol consumption by randomly assigned roommates has a strong effect on the academic performance of males but not females. Similarly, Katz, Kling, and Liebman (2001) find that MTO reallocation led to a decline in behavior problems among boys in both the experimental and Section 8 comparison groups but had no noticeable impact on girls. Kling, Liebman, and Katz (2007) conclude that female and male youth in the MTO treatment group responded to similar new neighborhood environments in different ways along various dimensions.

[31] We compute an indicator variable using unique case numbers that identify individuals convicted for the same crime and same type of crime.

but 75% resided in the same municipality of residence in the year of committing the crime, which is our neighborhood measure.

To investigate further whether our results are driven by the largest (and most urban) municipalities, we exclude first, the five largest municipalities (Copenhagen, Frederiksberg, Aarhus, Odense and Aalborg), and second, municipalities with more than 45,000 inhabitants (the 22 largest municipalities). The estimates in panel C and D are similar and – if anything – slightly larger than those in panel A.

To address the additional concern that our findings may be driven by the shares of immigrants who belong to the same ethnic group, we also investigate the impact of ethnic group crime on criminal behavior, conditional not only on the overall share of immigrants and descendants in the assignment area in the assignment year but also on the share of co-nationals. These results, reported in panel E, again suggest that including this variable has almost no effect on the coefficient estimates. In panel F, we report the results once the unemployment rate in the assignment area at the assignment date is included as an additional regressor. This inclusion barely affects our estimates. Since family size may predict location (see Table 1), we present in Panel G results where we restrict our sample to the model family size (2-3 siblings). This reduces our sample by more than one half. Point estimates are again similar, but with larger standard errors. Further estimations (not reported) using additional area characteristics like the share of lone mothers, the share of teenage mothers, or indices of inequality also lead to very similar estimates of the youth crime conviction rates.[32]

Crime-specific responses and crime-specific convictions: In Table 5, we report estimates for the probability of conviction in age range 15-21 when neighborhood youth crime conviction rates are broken down by crime categories, thereby distinguishing between youth conviction rates for violent crimes, property crimes, drug crimes, and other offenses. Here, we normalize every youth crime conviction rate by its standard deviation. The results indicate that it is mainly youth *violent* crime conviction rates that affect individual criminal behavior in each of the three age ranges, and coefficients for

---

[32] To further check whether our results are driven by one particular refugee group, we re-estimate our basic specification leaving out one minority group at a time. Again, the basic results remain unchanged (results not reported).

this crime category are precisely estimated.[33] The effect of youth property crime conviction rates is somewhat smaller but not statistically significant.

We therefore wonder whether the type of neighborhood crime convictions has a different effect on the different types of crime for which young offenders are convicted. Regressing convictions for each specific crime type on crime specific conviction rates, we find that the youth crime conviction rate for violent crimes does affect conviction probabilities for violent crimes, property crimes, and drug crimes while the effect of youth property crime conviction rates is smaller and only significantly different from zero in one case (see Table A11 in the appendix). Taken together, then, these results suggest that it is predominantly youth violent crime conviction rates that affect individual criminal behavior later on.

B. Mechanisms

We now turn to an assessment of the possible mechanisms that link neighborhood crime at assignment, and later criminal behavior. Our results in the previous section suggest that it seems unlikely that institutions or neighborhood culture, correlated with both municipality crime rates and individual's criminal behavior later in life, drive our results. We now pursue this further. We argue that – if social interaction is a main channel that relates the two – then what should matter for later criminal behavior is not the crimes committed in the assignment neighborhood, but the criminals who actually live in that neighborhood. Also, if social interaction is an important transmission channel, it should be youth crime conviction rates, and not overall or adult crime conviction rates, that affect later criminal behavior. We further assess whether convicted criminals in the assignment area who are possibly easier to interact with – such as those who are from the same ethnic group as the assignee– have a more pronounced effect on individuals' criminal behavior later in life. Finally, we investigate at which assignment age exposure to neighborhood crime matters most for later criminal delinquency.

---

[33] As seen from Table A10 in the appendix, the violent youth crime conviction rate also significantly influences the number of convictions in age range 15-21, while the effects of other types of youth crime conviction rates are insignificant.

Table 6 reports estimation results for different measures of neighborhood crime, all standardized by the standard deviation of the respective crime measure. Specifically, the table reports the outcomes for specifications (4) and (5) from Table 3 for the probability of conviction in the 15-21 age range.[34] The estimates in panels A and B replicate those in Tables 3 and 5 (for overall and violent youth crime conviction rates). In panels C and D, we condition on two additional crime measures frequently used in the literature: the number of reported crimes per capita and the number of reported violent crimes per 10,000 inhabitants. The coefficient estimates for reported crimes are small with large standard errors, and the estimates for reported violent crimes are insignificant for the second specification (as they are for the number of convictions, see Table A12). Ludwig and Kling (2007) find also no statistically significant effect of beat violent crime on arrests of male youth in MTO. These estimates therefore provide little evidence that children allocated to areas with higher crime rates are more likely to be convicted for a crime later in life. Thus, it is the share of criminals who live in the neighborhood, rather than the crimes committed, that seems to matter for later criminal behavior.

To investigate this further, in panels E and F, we report the results conditioned on both youth crime conviction rates and reported crimes, reported first for all crimes and then separately for violent crimes. Conditional on the share of youth convicted for a crime, the rates of committed crimes do not affect criminal behavior: the estimated coefficients on rates of crimes committed are small, with varying signs, and never close to statistically significant, while the estimated parameters on the youth conviction rate are very similar to those in panels A and B.[35]

In panels G and H, we report the findings conditioned on youth conviction rates and overall conviction rates (including convictions of individuals over 25) for all crimes (panel G) and for violent crimes only (panel H). The coefficients on the youth crime conviction rates are again similar to those in panels A and B, while the coefficients on the overall (violent) crime conviction rates (which pick up the effect of the conviction rates for individuals 25+) remain small and insignificant. It is thus young criminals living in

---

[34] Estimates for the number of convictions in the 15-21 age range are shown in Table A12 in the appendix.

[35] These specifications also address another important issue: resource swamping, which may lead to a correlation between crime rates and individual criminal behavior if an increase in crime reduces the resources available for crime investigation. Although our policing measures address this issue, the specifications in panels E and F should address any remaining concern.

the neighborhood at assignment that matter for later criminal convictions, which is compatible with social interaction being an important channel of transmission.[36]

Overall, these results suggest that when studying the effect of neighborhood crime on criminal behavior, it matters how criminal context is measured. One reason why measures of reported crime per capita may only incompletely capture the criminal environment to which young people are exposed is that they do not allow distinction between neighborhood crime intensity by the age range of offenders. Further, measures of reported crimes per capita may be a noisy proxy for the criminal environment to which young people are exposed, due to e.g. different degrees of repeat offending across neighborhoods (see Table 2), or criminals travelling to commit crime.[37]

If social interaction is a main channel through which neighborhood crime affects criminal behavior later in life, then it is reasonable to expect that young men will be more affected by criminals from their own ethnic group with whom they have more communication and interaction opportunities. In Table 7, we report the results for the conviction probability in the 15-21 age range of additionally conditioning on conviction rates of different origin groups, unconditional (upper panel) and conditional (lower panel) on municipality of assignment fixed effects. Specifically, we condition in addition on the crime conviction rates of young offenders who are immigrants or descendents of immigrants (column (2)), belong to a minority group from one of the eight refugee origin countries (column (3)), belong to the same origin country group as the respondent (columns (4) and (5)), and are from a minority group that belongs to one of the eight refugee origin countries but not to the respondent's group (column (5)). Each group-specific conviction rate is normalized by the group-specific standard deviation. The coefficient estimates on these additional variables measure the impact of the youth crime

---

[36] We have also estimated the effect of neighborhood crime on criminal behavior (measured as convictions) of the parents of our sample individuals, seven years after assignment (21.8% of fathers, and 14.9% of mothers carry a conviction at that point). None of the crime measures has any effect, which excludes intergenerational transmission as a possible mechanism linking neighborhood youth crime, and later criminal behavior (see Hjalmarsson and Lindquist, 2012). It also shows that it is young people who are affected by youth crime in the neighborhood.

[37] Some evidence for travels to crime in Denmark is given by Sorensen (2007) who reports that the average journey of crime for burglary was 14 km, with a median of about 5 km, using detailed administrative data for 2002/2003.

conviction rate for any of the respective groups, over and above the effect of the overall youth crime conviction rate.[38]

The inclusion of these additional variables barely changes the coefficient estimates of the overall youth crime conviction rates, and the youth crime conviction rate of other minority or immigrant groups does not additionally explain conviction probabilities. On the other hand, the youth crime conviction rates of co-nationals clearly affect later criminal behavior, over and above the effect of the overall share of convicted criminals. Whereas the coefficients on the overall share remain basically unchanged, a one standard deviation increase in the share of criminals from the same ethnic group increases conviction probabilities by another 2 percentage points (or about 4%).

Because the children in our sample are assigned to neighborhoods at different ages between 0 and 14 years, it is likely that the influence of neighborhood crime on young people's criminal behavior depends on how receptive they are to outside influences at assignment, which in turn may depend on their age at that point. To investigate this, we break the assignment age down into three categories: individuals assigned between 0 and 5 years (i.e., before starting primary school at age 6), individuals assigned between 6 and 9 years, and individuals assigned between 10 and 14 years of age, which produces three groups of 1,014, 1,466, and 1,945 individuals, respectively (see Table A14 in the appendix).

Table A15 in the appendix reports the results for convictions in these three age ranges, again based on Specifications (4) and (5) from Table 3. Overall, the results suggest that those 10 to 14 years old at assignment are most affected by the neighborhood conviction rate, while point estimates for individuals assigned between age 6 and 9 are similar to the overall estimates in Table 3 for crimes committed in the 15–21 and 18–21 age ranges, and for individuals assigned before age 6, the estimates are generally small and have large standard errors. However, care has to be taken when interpreting these results. Differences in assignment age also change the potential years of exposure to neighborhood crime, so that the estimates we present are a combination of group differences in potential years of exposure and age at assignment.

---

[38] As shown in Table A13 in the appendix, similar findings are obtained for the number of convictions.

C. Neighborhood Crime and Longer Term Outcomes

The final question we address is the effect of assignment to a high crime area on longer term outcomes, and we focus here on employment, and educational achievement of male individuals.[39] Although most papers focus on the effect of education on crime (see e.g. Jacob and Lefgen, 2003; Lochner and Moretti, 2004; Machin, Maie and Vujic, 2011), it may also be that growing up in a high crime area affects scholastic achievements. This could be through criminal engagement,[40] or through peer- or role model effects. Given the age structure of the assignees in our data and the period of the policy, this assessment is at this time only possible for a subset of men in our sample, as the last wave of administrative registers is 2006 and only 56% of the male sample has turned 25 by that date. For those, we monitor whether they have completed an upper-secondary or tertiary education, have joined the labor market, or are inactive. In Table 8, we investigate three outcomes: Whether the individual has obtained an upper-secondary or tertiary education (panel A), whether the individual is active (i.e. enrolled in education or employed) (panel A), and – considering only those who are not in education – whether the individual is employed (panel B). As this sample is only a subset of the sample we used before, we also report in the first row of each panel the effect of the youth violent crime conviction rate in the assignment area on the conviction probability at age 15-21. In the first two columns, we report regressions when individuals are 25 years old. In the next two columns, we pool observations for each individual for ages 23-25. For this specification, we allow for individual random effects. As before, we report results with, and without municipality fixed effects.

The effects of the youth violent crime conviction rate on conviction probabilities are similar (and possibly slightly larger) than those we report for the overall sample, as the estimates in the first row of each panel show. The youth violent crime conviction rate in the assignment area has no effect on the probability to have obtained an upper-secondary or tertiary education by age 23-25 (panel A). However, estimates point at those assigned to areas with higher violent youth crime conviction rates being less likely to be

---

[39] In an early paper, Grogger (1995) estimates the effects of arrests on employment and earnings in a non-experimental setting, and concludes that effects are moderate and short-lived.
[40] Hjalmarsson (2008) shows that the times caught committing crime and the amount of time spent in prison both increase the likelihood of becoming a high school dropout.

active (i.e. enrolled in education, or working), and – among those who are not in education (panel B) – less likely to be employed.[41] Although most of the coefficients are not precisely estimated, they are all similar in magnitude. Taking the estimates at face value, results in panel B suggests that an increase in the youth violent crime conviction rate by one standard deviation decreases the probability to be employed in the age range 23-25 by 1.8 percentage points (or 2.8 percent, given that 64% of this subsample is active). Thus, exposure to a high share of criminals living in one's neighborhood may have important consequences for other long-term outcomes of young men, either through their own criminal behavior, their contact with delinquent youth in general, or other mechanisms. This possibility raises interesting avenues for future research.

IV. CONCLUSION

To answer the question of whether exposure to neighborhood crime during childhood affects later criminal behavior, this paper draws on an exceptional spatial allocation experiment with refugee families in Denmark, whose quasi-randomness offers a unique solution to the fundamental methodological problem of endogenous neighborhood selection. We find strong evidence that the share of convicted criminals in the area at assignment affects later crime conviction probabilities, as well as the number of crimes for which a young man is convicted. We find no such effects, however, for females. It is the share of offenders convicted for crimes committed in the neighborhood that affects later crime conviction rates, in particular conviction rates for violent crimes among those in the under-26 age group. We detect no effects of other crime measures such as the rate of reported crimes. This emphasizes that it is the share of criminals living in the area, and not the rate of committed crimes, that affects later criminal engagement, which speaks in favor of social interaction as a key factor linking neighborhood crime with later criminal behavior.

Our findings provide additional evidence in support of this hypothesis: First, it is the crime conviction rate of youth that affect criminal behavior later in life. Crime

---

[41] One reason for the employment effects may be that individuals who are convicted for a crime between age 15 and 21 are still incarcerated. This is unlikely to affect employment rates after age 23 (for convictions received before age 22), however, as prison sentences administered to individuals in that age range are very short in Denmark: Based on data from Statistics Denmark (2005, p. 79), we calculated the average length of unsuspended prison sentences for this age range to be 5 months.

conviction rates of older individuals have no effect. Second, the youth crime conviction rates of individuals from the same ethnic group, with whom contact and interaction is likely to be easier and more frequent, matter more for individual convictions. Third, the age range in which assignees are most susceptible to neighborhood crime is between 10 and 14, an age at which young men are particularly vulnerable to delinquent peer influence.

We further find some evidence that youth crime conviction rates in the assignment area at assignment reduce the probability to be employed or in education by age 25. Unfortunately, the young age of our sample does not allow us to explore more conclusively additional and longer-term outcomes at present.

We should finally note that the findings we present in this paper refer to a group of young men whose crime rates are higher than those of the overall population. Nevertheless, we believe not only that understanding criminal behavior and its sources matters most in groups like those studied here or investigated in the MTO experiments, but that the basic mechanisms that link neighborhood crime to criminal behavior, explored in this paper, are likely to be relevant for other population groups as well.

References

Bayer, Patrick, Randi Hjalmarsson, and David Pozen, "Building Criminal Capital behind Bars: Peer Effects in Juvenile Corrections," *Quarterly Journal of Economics*, 124 (2009), 105–147.

Becker, Gary S., and Kevin M. Murphy, *Social Economics*, (Chicago: University of Chicago Press, 2000).

Brooks-Gunn, Jeanne; Duncan Greg J.; Kato Klebanov, Pamela and Sealand, Naomi, "Do Neighborhoods Influence Child and Adolescent Development?" *American Journal of Sociology*, 99.2 (1993), 353–395.

Carrell, Scott E., and Mark L. Hoekstra, "Externalities in the Classroom: How Children Exposed to Domestic Violence Affect Everyone's Kids," *American Economic Journal: Applied Economics*, 2.1 (2010), 211–228.

Case, Anne C., and Lawrence F. Katz, "The Company You Keep: The Effects of Family and Neighborhood on Disadvantaged Youths," NBER Working Paper no. 3705, 1991.

Chung, Kim-Sau, "Role Models and Arguments for Affirmative Action", *American Economic Review*, 90 (2000), pp. 640-648

Clampet-Lundquist, S., K. Edin, J.R. Kling, and G.J. Duncan, "Moving Teenagers Out of High-Risk Neighborhoods: How Girls Fare Better than Boys", American Journal of Sociology 116.4 (2011), pp. 1154-1189.

Cook, Philip J., and Kristin A. Goss, "A Selective Review of the Social Contagion Literature," unpublished working paper, Sanford Institute of Policy Studies, Duke University, 1996.

Currie, Janet, and Erdal Tekin, "Understanding the Cycle: Childhood Maltreatment and Future Crime," *Journal of Human Resources*, 47.2 (2012), 509-549.

Danish Refugee Council, *Annual Report*, 1986–1996.

Danish Refugee Council, *Administrativ Statistik* [Administrative statistics], 1992–1997.

Danish Refugee Council, Central Integration Unit (CIU), *Dansk Flygtningehjælps integrationsarbejde* [Danish Refugee Council Integration Policy], 1996.

Deming, David J., "Better Schools, Less Crime?" *Quarterly Journal of Economics,* 126 (2011), 2063–2115.

Edin, Per-Anders, Peter Fredriksson, and Olof Aslund, "Ethnic Enclaves and the Economic Success of Immigrants: Evidence from a Natural Experiment," *Quarterly Journal of Economics*, 118.1 (2003), 329–357.

Fougère, Denis, Francis Kramarz, and Julien Pouget, "Youth Unemployment and Crime in France,"*Journal of the European Economic Association,* 7.5 (2009), 909-938.

Glaeser, Edward L., Bruce Sacerdote, and José A. Scheinkman, "Crime and Social Interactions," *Quarterly Journal of Economics*, 111 (1996), 507–548.

Glaeser, Edward L., and Bruce Sacerdote, "Why Is There More Crime in Cities?" *Journal of Political Economy*, 107 (1999), 225–258.

Glaeser, Edward L., Bruce Sacerdote, and José A. Scheinkman, "The Social Multiplier," *Journal of the European Economic Association*, 1.2-3 (2003), 345–353.

Gould, Eric D., Victor Lavy, and M. Daniele Paserman, "Immigrating to Opportunity: Estimating the Effects of School Quality Using a Natural Experiment on Ethiopians in Israel," *Quarterly Journal of Economics*, 119.2 (2004), 489–526.

Gould, Eric D., Victor Lavy, and M. Daniele Paserman, "Sixty Years after the Magic Carpet Ride: Long-Run Effect of the Early Childhood Environment on Social and Economic Outcomes," *Review of Economic Studies*, 78.3 (2011), 938-973.

Gould, Eric D., Bruce Weinberg, and David B. Mustard, "Crime Rates and Local Labor Market Opportunities in the United States: 1977–1997," *Review of Economics and Statistics*, 84.1 (2002), 45–61.

Grogger, Jeffrey, "The Effect of Arrests on the Employment and Earnings of Young Men", *Quarterly Journal of Economics*, 110.1 (1995), 51-71.

Grogger, Jeffrey, "Market Wages and Youth Crime," *Journal of Labor Economics*, 16.4 (1998), 756–791.

Hjalmarsson, Randi, and Matthew Lindquist, "Like Godfather, Like Son: Exploring the Intergenerational Nature of Crime", *Journal of Human Resources*, 47.2 (2012), 550-882.

Hjalmarsson, Randi, "Criminal Justice Involvement and High School Completion", *Journal of Urban Economics*, 63 (2008), 613-630

Ingoldsby, Erin M., and Daniel S. Shaw, "Neighborhood Contextual Factors and Early-Starting Antisocial Pathways," *Clinical Child and Family Psychology Review*, 5 (2002), 21–55.

Jacob, Brian and L. Lefgren "Are Idle Hands the Devil's Workshop? Incapacitation, Concentration and Juvenile Crime," *American Economic Review*, 93 (2003), 1560-1577.

Katz, Lawrence F., Jeffrey R. Kling, and Jeffrey B. Liebman, "Moving to Opportunity in Boston: Early Results of a Randomized Mobility Experiment," *Quarterly Journal of Economics*, 116.2 (2001), 607–654.

Kemper. T.D., "Reference Groups, Socialization, and Achievement," *American Sociological Review,* 33 (1968), 57-78.

Kling, Jeffrey R., Jeffrey B. Liebman, and Lawrence F. Katz, "Experimental Analysis of Neighborhood Effects." *Econometrica*, 75 (2007), 83–119.

Kling, Jeffrey R., Jens Ludwig, and Lawrence F. Katz, "Neighborhood Effects on Crime for Female and Male Youth: Evidence from a Randomized Housing Voucher Experiment," *Quarterly Journal of Economics,* 120.1 (2005), 87–131.

Kremer, Michael, and Dan M. Levy, "Peer Effects and Alcohol Use among College Students," Journal of Economic Perspectives 22.3 (2008), pp. 189-206.

Kyvsgaard, Britta, *The Criminal Career: The Danish Longitudinal Study* (City: Cambridge University Press, 2003).

Levitt, Steven D., "Using Electoral Cycles in Police Hiring to Estimate the Effect of Police on Crime," *American Economic Review*, 87.3 (1997), 270–290.

Levitt, Steven D., "Juvenile Crime and Punishment," *Journal of Political Economy*, 106 (1998), 1156-1185

Lochner, Lance, and Enrico Moretti, "The Effect of Education on Crime: Evidence from Prison Inmates, Arrests, and Self-Reports," *American Economic Review*, 94.1 (2004), 155–189.

Logan, J. R., and S. F. Messner, "Racial Residential Segregation and Suburban Violent Crime," *Social Science Quarterly*, 68.3 (1987), 510–527.

Ludwig, J., G. J. Duncan, and P. Hirschfield, "Urban Poverty and Juvenile Crime: Evidence from a Randomized Experiment," *Quarterly Journal of Economics*, 116 (2001), 655–679.

Ludwig, Jens, and Jeffrey R. Kling, "Is Crime Contagious?" *Journal of Law and Economics*, 50 (2007), 491–518.

Machin, Stephen, and Costas Meghir, "Crime and Economic Incentives," *Journal of Human Resources,* 39.4 (2004), 958–979.

Machin, Stephen, Olivier Marie and Suncica Vujic, "The Crime Reducing Effect of Education", *The Economic Journal*, 212 (2011), 463-484

Manski, Charles F. "identification of Endogenous Social Effects: The Reflection Problem. *The Review of Economic Studies* 60.3 (1993), 531-542

Manski, Charles F. "Economic Analysis of Social Interactions." *The Journal of Economic Perspectives* 14.3 (2000), 115-136.

Mears, Daniel P, Matthew Ploeger, and Mark Warr, "Explaining the Gender Gap in Delinquency: Peer Influence and Moral Evaluations of Behavior," *Journal of Research in Crime and Delinquency*, 35 (1998), 251–266.

Oreopoulos, Philip, "The Long-Run Consequences of Living in a Poor Neighborhood," *Quarterly Journal of Economics*, 118.4 (2003), 1533–1575.

Sacerdote, Bruce, "Peer Effects with Random Assignment: Results for Dartmouth roommates", *Quarterly Journal of Economics*, 116.2 (2001), 681-704.

Sanbonmatsu, L., J. Ludwig, L. F. Katz, L. A. Gennetian, G. J. Duncan, E. Adam, T. W. McDade, and S. T. Lindau, "Moving to Opportunity for Fair Housing Demonstration

Program: Final Impact Evaluation," (2011), available at http://www.huduser.org/publications/pdf/MTOFHD_fullreport.pdf

Sorensen, David W.M. Kriminalitetsrejsen. Om indbrudstyves mobilitet. *Nordisk Tidsskrift for Kriminalvidenskab*, Årg. 1994, nr. 2 (2007), 143-169

Statistics Denmark, *Kriminalitet 2005* [Criminality 2005].

Statistical Yearbook [Statistisk Årbog] various years, Copenhagen: Statistics Denmark.

Steffensmeier, Darrel J., and Emilie A. Allan, "Gender and Crime: Toward a Gendered Theory of Female Offending," *Annual Review of Sociology*, 22 (1996), 459-487.

Table 1: Assignment location attributes and individual characteristics of assignees.

	Dependent variable: Different measures of crime in municipality of assignment					
	Youth crime conviction rate (%)	Youth violent crime conviction rate (%)	Overall crime conviction rate (%)	Overall violent crime conviction rate (%)	Number of reported crimes per capita (%)	Number of reported violent crimes per 10,000 inhabitants
	1	2	3	4	5	6

Panel A

Years of education Household head (ref. category: 0-9 years):

10-12 years	-0.002	0.003	-0.007	-0.000	-0.128	0.130
	(0.044)	(0.008)	(0.019)	(0.002)	(0.248)	(0.499)
More than 12 years	-0.019	0.003	-0.017	0.001	-0.192	0.013
	(0.049)	(0.009)	(0.021)	(0.002)	(0.277)	(0.558)
Unknown	0.006	0.002	0.001	0.001	0.127	0.557
	(0.045)	(0.008)	(0.020)	(0.002)	(0.256)	(0.515)
Age	0.002	-0.001*	0.001	-0.000	0.021*	0.020
	(0.002)	(0.000)	(0.001)	(0.000)	(0.009)	(0.019)
Number of children	-0.012	-0.002	-0.008*	-0.001	-0.127**	-0.208*
	(0.008)	(0.001)	(0.004)	(0.000)	(0.046)	(0.092)
Married	0.050	0.007	0.019	0.002	0.207	0.340
	(0.048)	(0.009)	(0.021)	(0.002)	(0.269)	(0.541)
Country of origin F.E.	Yes	Yes	Yes	Yes	Yes	Yes
Year of immigration F.E.	Yes	Yes	Yes	Yes	Yes	Yes
N			2,396			

Test of joint insignificance of educational attainment categories in linear regressions above

$F_{(3,2370)}$	0.12	0.04	0.38	0.15	0.79	0.65
Prob>F	0.95	0.9891	0.7686	0.9287	0.4999	0.5844

Test of joint insignificance of educational attainment dummies, age, number of children and married dummy in linear regressions above

$F_{(6,2370)}$	1.06	1.06	1.82	0.60	3.23	1.73
Prob>F	0.3840	0.3873	0.0905	0.7308	0.0036	0.1095

Panel B

Years of education Household head (ref. category: 0-9 years):

10-12 years	-0.003	-0.001	-0.002	-0.001	-0.047	0.162
	(0.018)	(0.006)	(0.005)	(0.001)	(0.089)	(0.259)
More than 12 years	-0.019	-0.007	-0.007	-0.001	-0.143	-0.256
	(0.020)	(0.006)	(0.006)	(0.001)	(0.100)	(0.291)
Unknown	0.002	0.004	-0.003	0.001	-0.004	0.286
	(0.018)	(0.006)	(0.005)	(0.001)	(0.092)	(0.267)
Age	0.000	-0.000	0.000	-0.000	0.006	-0.000
	(0.001)	(0.000)	(0.000)	(0.000)	(0.003)	(0.010)
Number of children	0.004	-0.001	0.002*	0.000	0.021	0.104*
	(0.003)	(0.001)	(0.001)	(0.000)	(0.017)	(0.049)
Married	0.012	0.007	0.002	0.000	0.072	-0.289
	(0.020)	(0.006)	(0.006)	(0.001)	(0.099)	(0.287)
Country of origin F.E.	Yes	Yes	Yes	Yes	Yes	Yes
Year of immigration F.E.	Yes	Yes	Yes	Yes	Yes	Yes
Municipality F.E.	Yes	Yes	Yes	Yes	Yes	Yes
N			2,396			

Test of joint insignificance of educational attainment categories in linear regressions above						
F(3,2174)	0.6	1.49	0.49	1.77	1.04	1.79
Prob>F	0.6141	0.2162	0.6923	0.1516	0.3719	0.1478

Test of joint insignificance of educational attainment dummies, age, number of children and married dummy in linear regressions above						
F(6,2174)	0.70	0.94	1.09	1.13	1.58	1.81
Prob>F	0.6523	0.4660	0.3685	0.3403	0.1476	0.0940

Note: **: P<0.01, *:P<0.05. Administrative register information from Statistics Denmark for household heads of refugee children. The sample of refugee children (henceforth referred to as the balanced sample of refugee children) are children of immigrants from a refugee-sending country (Iraq, Iran, Vietnam, Sri Lanka, Lebanon, Ethiopia, Afghanistan, Somalia) in the 1986-1998 period, who immigrated before age 15 and at most one year later than the refugee parent(s) and who are observed annually up to age 21. Reported coefficients are based on linear regressions of municipality of assignment crime rates in the year of assignment on individual characteristics in year of assignment.

Table 2: Summary statistics, charges and convictions.

	Refugee children		
	All	Men	Women
Panel A: Age range 15-21			
Charged with a criminal offence	0.376	0.545	0.165
	(0.484)	(0.498)	(0.372)
Convicted of a criminal offence	0.314	0.459	0.134
	(0.464)	(0.498)	(0.341)
Convicted of violent assualt	0.104	0.180	0.009
	(0.305)	(0.384)	(.093)
Convicted of a property offence	0.247	0.347	0.122
	(0.431)	(0.476)	(0.328)
Convicted of a drugs crime	0.054	0.092	0.006
	(0.225)	(0.289)	(.075)
Convicted of another offence	0.090	0.154	0.011
	(0.286)	(0.361)	(0.103)
Number of charges	3.163	5.419	0.356
	(10.785)	(14.006)	(1.684)
Number of convictions	0.909	1.480	0.199
	(2.155)	(2.693)	(0.599)
N	4,425	2,453	1,972
Panel B: Age range 15-21			
Distribution of number of convictions:			
0 conviction	3,036	1,328	1,708
1 conviction	647	454	193
2 convictions	289	238	51
3 convictions	122	111	11
4 convictions	61	59	2
5 or more convictions	270	263	7
N	4,425	2,453	1,972
Panel C: Age range 15-17			
Charged with a criminal offence	0.251	0.374	0.098
	(0.408)	(0.464)	(.276)
Convicted of a criminal offence	0.211	0.314	0.083
	(0.408)	(0.464)	(0.276)
Number of charges	1.276	2.172	0.162
	(5.117)	(6.709)	(0.734)
Number of convictions	0.409	0.653	0.106
	(1.08)	(1.35)	(0.418)
N	4,425	2,453	1,972
Panel D: Age range 18-21			
Charged with a criminal offence	0.279	0.432	0.090
	(0.449)	(0.495)	(0.286)
Convicted of a criminal offence	0.217	0.338	0.066
	(0.412)	(0.473)	(0.248)
Number of charges	1.886	3.247	0.192
	(6.935)	(9.018)	(1.259)
Number of convictions	0.500	0.827	0.093
	(1.32)	(1.65)	(0.438)
N	4,425	2,453	1,972

Note: Administrative register information from Statistics Denmark for the balanced sample of refugee children (described in the footnote to Table 1). Charge and conviction rates are calculated from the Central Police Register. Traffic offenses are excluded.

Table 3: Effect of a standard deviation increase in the youth crime conviction rate in the municipality of assignment in year of assignment on convictions.

Panel A: Men.	1	2	3	4	5
Convicted in age range					
15-21	0.019	0.017	0.023*	0.023*	0.043**
	(0.013)	(0.012)	(0.012)	(0.012)	(0.022)
15-17	0.017	0.015	0.014	0.014	0.027
	(0.013)	(0.012)	(0.013)	(0.013)	(0.019)
18-21	0.020*	0.019**	0.025**	0.023**	0.031
	(0.010)	(0.010)	(0.012)	(0.012)	(0.020)
Number of convictions in age range					
15-21	0.122**	0.113**	0.118*	0.106*	0.169*
	(0.058)	(0.052)	(0.062)	(0.063)	(0.097)
15-17	0.068**	0.061**	0.055*	0.050	0.098*
	(0.027)	(0.025)	(0.033)	(0.034)	(0.051)
18-21	0.054	0.052	0.063*	0.056	0.071
	(0.035)	(0.032)	(0.036)	(0.037)	(0.056)
Panel B: Women.	**1**	**2**	**3**	**4**	**5**
Convicted in age range					
15-21	-0.008	-0.004	0.002	0.001	0.031
	(0.007)	(0.007)	(0.010)	(0.010)	(0.020)
15-17	-0.005	-0.002	-0.002	-0.002	0.015
	(0.007)	(0.007)	(0.009)	(0.009)	(0.017)
18-21	-0.004	-0.001	0.005	0.003	0.018
	(0.005)	(0.006)	(0.008)	(0.008)	(0.018)
Number of convictions in age range					
15-21	0.001	0.018	0.022	0.008	0.095
	(0.014)	(0.021)	(0.033)	(0.035)	(0.084)
15-17	-0.004	0.003	-0.003	-0.009	0.048
	(0.008)	(0.011)	(0.018)	(0.019)	(0.044)
18-21	0.005	0.015	0.025	0.017	0.047
	(0.009)	(0.013)	(0.021)	(0.020)	(0.050)
Controls:					
Gender	Yes	Yes	Yes	Yes	Yes
Country of origin, year, and age at assignment FE; Family background, ln(size ethnic group DK)	No	Yes	Yes	Yes	Yes
Poverty rate, immigrant share, pop. Size, number of teacher hours/pupil, pupils/teacher ratio	No	No	Yes	Yes	Yes
Crime detection rate, police officers/1000	No	No	No	Yes	Yes
Municipality of assignment FE	No	No	No	No	Yes
N			4,425		

Note : ***p<0.01, **p<0.05, *p<0.10. Robust standard errors clustered by municipality of assignment (204 cells) are reported in parentheses. Administrative register information from Statistics Denmark for the balanced sample of refugee children (described in the footnote to Table 1). Family background and municipality of assignment characteristics refer to the year of assignment. Mean (standard deviation) of the youth crime conviction rate in the municipality of assignment (in %): 2.47 (0.70).

Table 4: Effect of a standard deviation increase in the youth crime conviction rate in the municipality of assignment in year of assignment on convictions. Robustness checks. Men.

	Convicted (or charged)		Number Convictions (or Charges)	
	15-21 age range		15-21 age range	
	1	2	3	4
Panel A: Dependent variable: crime conviction				
Youth crime conviction rate	0.023*	0.043**	0.106*	0.169*
	(0.012)	(0.022)	(0.063)	(0.097)
N			4,425	
Panel B: Dependent variable: crime charges				
Youth crime conviction rate	0.024**	0.036*	0.107	0.422
	(0.011)	(0.021)	(0.390)	(0.471)
N			4,425	
Panel C: Excluding the five largest municipalities				
Youth crime conviction rate	0.032**	0.060**	0.170**	0.235**
	(0.014)	(0.024)	(0.077)	(0.115)
N			3,035	
Panel D: Excluding the twenty-two largest municipalities				
Youth crime conviction rate	0.033*	0.074**	0.233**	0.329**
	(0.018)	(0.028)	(0.095)	(0.129)
N			2,254	
Panel E: Conditioning on the co-national share in the municipality of assignment				
Youth crime conviction rate	0.022*	0.045**	0.099	0.178*
	(0.012)	(0.022)	(0.063)	(0.095)
N			4,425	
Panel F: Conditioning on the unemployment rate in the municipality of assignment				
Youth crime conviction rate	0.020*	0.044**	0.087	0.168*
	(0.012)	(0.022)	(0.059)	(0.098)
N			4,425	
Panel G: Results using only observations for children with the modal number of siblings of 2-3				
Youth crime conviction rate	0.044**	0.061	0.151	0.178
	(0.020)	(0.042)	(0.105)	(0.220)
N			1,985	
Controls:				
As in Specification 4, Table 3	Yes	Yes	Yes	Yes
Municipality of assignment F.E.	No	Yes	No	Yes

Note: ***$p<0.01$, **$p<0.05$, *$p<0.10$. Robust standard errors clustered by the municipality of assignment (204 cells) are reported in parentheses. Administrative register information from Statistics Denmark for the balanced sample of refugee children (described in the footnote to Table 1). Family background and municipality of assignment characteristics refer to the year of assignment. Mean (standard deviation) of the youth crime conviction rate in municipality of assignment (in %): 2.47 (0.70).

Table 5: Effect of a standard deviation increase in type-specific youth crime conviction rates in the municipality of assignment in year of assignment on convictions. Men.

(In %)	15-21		15-17		18-21	
	1	2	3	4	5	6
Dependent variable: Convicted in age range						
Panel A						
Youth violent crime conviction rate	0.034***	0.045***	0.035***	0.046***	0.021**	0.024*
	(0.011)	(0.014)	(0.011)	(0.013)	(0.010)	(0.012)
Panel B						
Youth property crime conviction rate	0.016	0.029	0.008	0.009	0.017	0.019
	(0.012)	(0.021)	(0.013)	(0.019)	(0.011)	(0.019)
Panel C						
Youth drugs crime conviction rate	-0.011	-0.006	-0.015	0.005	0.003	0.002
	(0.013)	(0.018)	(0.012)	(0.016)	(0.013)	(0.017)
Panel D						
Youth conviction rate of other offences	0.021*	0.011	0.017	0.005	0.022*	0.017
	(0.012)	(0.016)	(0.011)	(0.015)	(0.011)	(0.015)
Controls:						
As in Specification 4, Table 3	Yes	Yes	Yes	Yes	Yes	Yes
Municipality of assignment FE	No	Yes	No	Yes	No	Yes
N			4,425			

Note: ***: $P<0.01$, **: $P<0.05$, *: $P<0.10$. Robust standard errors clustered by the municipality of assignment (204 cells) are reported in parentheses. Administrative register information from Statistics Denmark for the balanced sample of refugee children (described in the footnote to Table 1). Family background and municipality of assignment characteristics refer to the year of assignment. Mean (standard deviation) of type-specific youth crime conviction rates (of 15-25 year olds) in the municipality of assignment and year of assignment (in percentages) prior to standardization as deviations from the mean relative to the standard deviation: Violence assault: 0.286 (0.123), Property crime: 1.782 (0.528), Drugs offences: 0.301 (0.238) and other offences: 0.342 (0.159).

Table 6: Effect of a standard deviation increase in different crime measures in the municipality of assignment on the conviction probability. Men.

	Dependent variable: Convicted in 15-21 age range	
	1	2
Panel A		
Youth crime conviction rate	0.023*	0.043**
	(0.012)	(0.022)
Panel B		
Youth violent crime conviction rate	0.034***	0.045***
	(0.011)	(0.014)
Panel C		
Number of reported crimes per capita	0.011	-0.002
	(0.016)	(0.021)
Panel D		
Number of reported violent crimes per 10,000 inhabitants	0.027*	-0.000
	(0.014)	(0.018)
Panel E		
Youth crime conviction rate	0.022	0.045**
	(0.014)	(0.022)
Number of reported crimes per capita	-0.000	-0.008
	(0.017)	(0.022)
Panel F		
Youth violent crime conviction rate	0.030**	0.046***
	(0.012)	(0.014)
Number of reported violent crimes per 10,000 inhabitants	0.014	-0.015
	(0.015)	(0.018)
Panel G		
Youth crime conviction rate	0.033	0.044
	(0.022)	(0.028)
Overall crime conviction rate	-0.015	0.003
	(0.029)	(0.043)
Panel H		
Youth violent crime conviction rate	0.039**	0.061***
	(0.019)	(0.020)
Overall violent crime conviction rate	-0.007	-0.026
	(0.020)	(0.024)
Controls:		
As in Specification (4), Table 3	Yes	Yes
Municipality of assignment F.E.	No	Yes
N	4,425	

Note: ***p<0.01, **p<0.05, *p<0.10. Robust standard errors clustered by the municipality of assignment (204 cells) are reported in parentheses. Administrative register information from Statistics Denmark for the balanced sample of refugee children (described in the footnote to Table 1). Youth crime conviction rate (in percentages): 2.47 (0.70), overall crime conviction rate (in percentages): 0.95 (0.31), number of reported crimes per capita: 7.25 (3.17), number of reported violent crimes per 10,000 inhabitants: 17.16 (9.63), overall violent crime conviction rate (in percentages): 0.09 (0.03), youth violent crime conviction rate (in percentages): 0.29 (0.12).

Table 7: Effect of a standard deviation increase in different youth crime conviction rates on the conviction probability. Men.

	Dependent Variable: Convicted in the 15-21 age range				
	1	2	3	4	5
Youth crime conviction rate					
All	0.023*	0.028**	0.021*	0.022*	0.022*
	(0.012)	(0.013)	(0.012)	(0.013)	(0.013)
Immigrants and descendants		-0.013			
		(0.012)			
Immigrants and descendants from refugee-sending countries			0.006		
			(0.010)		
Co-nationals				0.023**	0.023**
				(0.010)	(0.010)
Immigrants and descendants from other refugee-sending countries					-0.010
					(0.008)
Controls:					
As in Specification (4), Table 3	Yes	Yes	Yes	Yes	Yes
Municipality of assignment F.E.	No	No	No	No	No
N			4,425		
Youth crime conviction rate					
All	0.043**	0.052**	0.043**	0.042*	0.042*
	(0.022)	(0.021)	(0.021)	(0.022)	(0.021)
Immigrants and descendants		-0.022*			
		(0.013)			
Immigrants and descendants from refugee-sending countries			0.002		
			(0.013)		
Co-nationals				0.023**	0.023**
				(0.010)	(0.010)
Immigrants and descendants from other refugee-					-0.008
					(0.013)
Controls:					
As in Specification (4), Table 3	Yes	Yes	Yes	Yes	Yes
Municipality of assignment F.E.	Yes	Yes	Yes	Yes	Yes
N			4,425		

Note: ***$p<0.01$, **$p<0.05$, *$p<0.10$. Robust standard errors clustered by the municipality of assignment (204 cells) are reported in parentheses. Administrative register information from Statistics Denmark for the balanced sample of refugee children (described in the footnote to Table 1). Mean (standard deviation) of the different youth crime rates (in %) in the municipality of assignment before standardization as deviations from the mean relative to the standard deviation: Youth crime conviction rate: 2.47 (0.70), youth crime conviction rate of immigrants and descendants: 3.86 (2.55), youth crime conviction rate of immigrants and descendants from refugee-sending countries in sample: 4.64 (5.65), youth crime conviction rate of co-nationals: 4.99 (5.65), youth crime conviction rate of immigrants and descendants from other refugee-sending countries: 4.46 (7.36).

Table 8: Effect of a crime conviction by age 21 on attainment of an upper-secondary or tertiary education and on being active and employed. Men aged 23-25.

	Age 25		Age 23-25	
	1	2	3	4
Panel A: Dependent variables: Indicators for attainment of an upper-secondary or tertiary education and for being active (employed or enrolled in education). OLS.				
Effect of youth violent crime conviction rate in municipality of assignment on having been convicted of a crime committed between age 15 and 21	0.040***	0.045**	0.039***	0.051***
	(0.015)	(0.020)	(0.013)	(0.015)
Effect of the youth violent crime conviction rate in the municipality of assignment on attainment of an upper-secondary or tertiary education	-0.003	0.001	-0.004	-0.003
	(0.014)	(0.022)	(0.011)	(0.015)
Effect of the youth violent crime conviction rate in the municipality of assignment on being active	-0.014	-0.014	-0.016*	-0.007
	(0.013)	(0.019)	(0.009)	(0.012)
N	2,480		9,101	
Panel B: Dependent variable: Employed versus inactive. OLS.				
Effect of youth violent crime conviction rate in municipality of assignment on having been convicted of a crime committed between age 15 and 21	0.042***	0.037*	0.041***	0.046***
	(0.015)	(0.020)	(0.013)	(0.015)
Effect of the youth violent crime conviction rate in the municipality of assignment on being employed	-0.019	-0.016	-0.018*	-0.011
	(0.014)	(0.021)	(0.010)	(0.014)
N	2,223		7,956	
Controls:				
As in Specification (4), Table 3	Yes	Yes	Yes	Yes
Municipality of assignm. FE	No	Yes	No	Yes
Individual random effects	No	No	Yes	Yes

Note: ***: P<0.01, **:P<0.05, *:P<0.10. Robust standard errors clustered by the municipality of assignment (204 cells) are reported in parentheses. Administrative register information from Statistics Denmark for the balanced sample of refugee children (described in the footnote to Table 1). Family background and municipality of assignment characteristics refer to the year of assignment. Mean (standard deviation) of the youth violent crime conviction rate in the municipality of assignment and year of assignment (in percentages) prior to standardization as deviations from the mean relative to the standard deviation: 0.29 (0.12). 54% of individuals in the sample of 25 year olds are employed, 26.6% of individuals are enrolled in education, 64.4% are active (employed or enrolled in education) and 41.0% have completed an upper-secondary or tertiary education.

Appendix

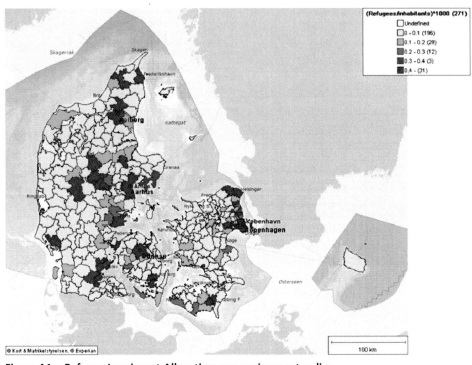

Figure A1a: Refugee Immigrant Allocation, pre-assignment policy

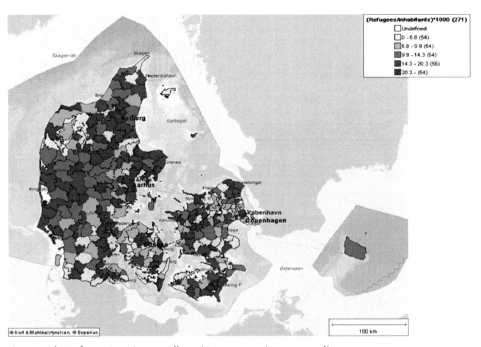

Figure A1b: Refugee Immigrant Allocation, post-assignment policy

Table A1: Kaplan-Meier survival rates in the municipality of assignment.

Year	Kaplan-Meier survival rate
0	1.000
1	0.761
2	0.705
3	0.656
4	0.609
5	0.579
6	0.546
7	0.515
8	0.491
9	0.466
10	0.439
11	0.415
12	0.392
13	0.367
14	0.340
15	0.307
16	0.272
17	0.238
18	0.217
19	0.184
20	0.147

Note: Administrative register information from Statistics Denmark for the balanced sample of refugee children (described in the footnote to Table 1).

Table A2.a: Assignment location attributes and individual characteristics of assignees in the year of assignment. Sample of household heads of children in the full sample of refugee children.

| | Dependent variable: Different measures of crime in municipality of assignment | | | | | | | | | | | |
| | Youth crime conviction rate (%) | | Youth violent crime conviction rate (%) | | Overall crime conviction rate (%) | | Overall violent crime conviction rate (%) | | Number of reported crimes per capita (%) | | Number of reported violent crimes per 10,000 inhabitants | |
	1	2	3	4	5	6	7	8	9	10	11	12
Years of education (ref. category: 0-9 years):												
10-12 years	-0.042	-0.012	-0.001	0.001	-0.019	-0.003	-0.001	-0.001	-0.168	0.031	0.063	0.334
	(0.041)	(0.016)	(0.007)	(0.005)	(0.018)	(0.005)	(0.002)	(0.001)	(0.230)	(0.083)	(0.460)	(0.243)
More than 12 years	-0.031	-0.018	0.001	-0.003	-0.022	-0.006	-0.000	-0.001	-0.221	-0.119	-0.050	-0.155
	(0.047)	(0.018)	(0.008)	(0.006)	(0.020)	(0.005)	(0.002)	(0.001)	(0.260)	(0.095)	(0.520)	(0.276)
Unknown	-0.021	-0.003	-0.001	0.006	-0.007	-0.004	-0.001	0.001	0.100	0.063	0.381	0.374
	(0.042)	(0.016)	(0.007)	(0.005)	(0.018)	(0.005)	(0.002)	(0.001)	(0.232)	(0.084)	(0.464)	(0.245)
Age	0.002	0.000	-0.000	-0.000	0.001	0.000	-0.000	-0.000	0.011	0.004	0.004	-0.006
	(0.002)	(0.001)	(0.000)	(0.000)	(0.001)	(0.000)	(0.000)	(0.000)	(0.008)	(0.003)	(0.017)	(0.009)
Number of children	-0.016*	0.004	-0.002	-0.000	-0.010**	0.002*	-0.001	0.000	-0.164**	0.012	-0.274**	0.049
	(0.008)	(0.003)	(0.001)	(0.001)	(0.003)	(0.001)	(0.000)	(0.000)	(0.042)	(0.016)	(0.084)	(0.045)
Married	0.023	-0.006	-0.001	0.000	0.019	-0.002	0.001	0.000	0.296	0.060	0.484	-0.190
	(0.044)	(0.018)	(0.008)	(0.006)	(0.019)	(0.005)	(0.002)	(0.001)	(0.247)	(0.091)	(0.493)	(0.264)
Country of origin F.E.	Yes	Yes	Yes	Yes	Yes	Yes	Yes	Yes	Yes	Yes	Yes	Yes
Year of immigration F.E.	Yes	Yes	Yes	Yes	Yes	Yes	Yes	Yes	Yes	Yes	Yes	Yes
Municipality F.E.	No	Yes	No	Yes	No	Yes	No	Yes	No	Yes	No	Yes
N						2,882						
Panel B: Test of joint insignificance of educational attainment categories in linear regressions above												
F(3,2856) or F(3,2654)	0.38	0.48	0.03	1.31	0.69	0.42	0.16	1.42	1.06	1.91	0.46	2.49
Prob>F	0.7709	0.6927	0.9921	0.269	0.5577	0.741	0.9209	0.2353	0.3643	0.1251	0.708	0.0587
Panel C: Test of joint insignificance of educational attainment dummies, age, number of children and married dummy in linear regressions above												
F(6,2856) or F(6,2654)	1.52	0.63	0.86	0.79	2.50	1.22	0.94	1.16	3.82	1.54	2.19	1.54
Prob>F	0.1683	0.7031	0.5225	0.5811	0.0203	0.2948	0.4625	0.3222	0.0008	0.1620	0.0412	0.1595

Note: **: P<0.01; *: P<0.05. Administrative register information from Statistics Denmark for household heads of children in the full sample of refugee children. The full sample of refugee children are children of immigrants from one of the following refugee-sending country: Iraq, Iran, Vietnam, Sri Lanka, Lebanon, Ethiopia, Afghanistan or Somalia, who immigrated before age 15 in the 1986-1998 period and at most one year later than the refugee parent(s) and who turn 21 years old in the period 1986-2006. Linear regression of municipality of assignment crime rates in the year of assignment on individual characteristics in year of assignment. 22.6% of household heads are female.

Table A2.b: Location assignment of refugee children and personal characteristics: Linear regression of municipality of assignment crime rates in year of assignment on gender, age at assignment and family characteristics in year of assignment. Sample of refugee children.

Dependent variable: Different measures of crime in municipality of assignment

	Youth crime conviction rate (%)		Youth violent crime conviction rate (%)		Overall crime conviction rate (%)		Overall violent crime conviction rate (%)		Number of reported crimes per capita (%)		Number of reported violent crimes per 10,000 inhabitants	
	1	2	3	4	5	6	7	8	9	10	11	12
					Panel A: OLS estimates							
Child is female	0.059**	0.009	0.003	-0.002	0.017*	0.004	0.001	-0.000	0.041	-0.000	0.102	0.046
	(0.020)	(0.008)	(0.004)	(0.003)	(0.008)	(0.003)	(0.001)	(0.001)	(0.109)	(0.041)	(0.230)	(0.111)
Child's age at assignment	-0.002	-0.002	-0.000	-0.000	-0.001	-0.001	-0.000	-0.000	-0.005	-0.001	-0.048	-0.029
	(0.004)	(0.001)	(0.001)	(0.000)	(0.002)	(0.000)	(0.000)	(0.000)	(0.021)	(0.007)	(0.038)	(0.019)
Years of education of household head (ref. category: 0-9 years):												
10-12 years	0.048	-0.017	0.008	-0.001	0.012	-0.005	0.002	-0.001	-0.037	-0.122	0.319	-0.146
	(0.051)	(0.019)	(0.009)	(0.006)	(0.021)	(0.006)	(0.002)	(0.001)	(0.272)	(0.098)	(0.530)	(0.269)
More than 12 years	-0.017	-0.029	0.007	-0.006	-0.016	-0.011	0.002	-0.001	-0.211	-0.218	0.201	-0.515
	(0.057)	(0.023)	(0.010)	(0.007)	(0.024)	(0.007)	(0.003)	(0.001)	(0.304)	(0.114)	(0.587)	(0.311)
Unknown	0.031	-0.004	0.006	0.004	0.011	-0.006	0.002	0.001	0.218	-0.066	0.724	-0.027
	(0.052)	(0.019)	(0.009)	(0.006)	(0.021)	(0.006)	(0.002)	(0.001)	(0.280)	(0.097)	(0.520)	(0.259)
Household head is married	0.024	-0.020	0.005	0.003	0.018	-0.007	0.002	-0.000	0.167	-0.030	0.134	-0.704*
	(0.052)	(0.019)	(0.010)	(0.007)	(0.023)	(0.007)	(0.002)	(0.002)	(0.300)	(0.113)	(0.594)	(0.319)
Age of household head	0.005*	0.001	-0.000	0.000	0.002*	0.000	0.000	-0.000	0.030**	0.005	0.045*	0.007
	(0.002)	(0.001)	(0.000)	(0.000)	(0.001)	(0.000)	(0.000)	(0.000)	(0.011)	(0.004)	(0.022)	(0.011)
Number of siblings	-0.020	0.003	-0.000	0.002	-0.008	0.001	-0.000	0.000	-0.115*	-0.025	-0.162	-0.014
	(0.010)	(0.004)	(0.002)	(0.001)	(0.005)	(0.001)	(0.001)	(0.000)	(0.056)	(0.020)	(0.113)	(0.055)
Country of origin F.E.	Yes	Yes	Yes	Yes	Yes	Yes	Yes	Yes	Yes	Yes	Yes	Yes
Year of immigration F.E.	Yes	Yes	Yes	Yes	Yes	Yes	Yes	Yes	Yes	Yes	Yes	Yes
Municipality F.E.	No	Yes	No	Yes	No	Yes	No	Yes	No	Yes	No	Yes
N					4,425							

To be continued.

Table A2.b (continued): Location assignment of refugee children and personal characteristics: Linear regression of municipality of assignment crime rates in year of assignment on gender, age at assignment and family characteristics in year of assignment. Sample of refugee children.

	Youth crime conviction rate (%)		Youth violent crime conviction rate (%)		Overall crime conviction rate (%)		Overall violent crime conviction rate (%)		Number of reported crimes per capita (%)		Number of reported violent crimes per 10,000 inhabitants	
	Dependent variable: Different measures of crime in municipality of assignment											
	1	2	3	4	5	6	7	8	9	10	11	12
Panel B: Test of joint insignificance of household head educational attainment categories in linear regressions above												
F(3,2407)	0.79	0.85	0.29	1.16	0.81	0.71	0.38	1.66	0.98	1.42	0.83	1.29
Prob>F	0.5011	0.4650	0.8359	0.3237	0.4872	0.5443	0.7662	0.1734	0.3992	0.2354	0.4798	0.2766
Panel C: Test of joint insignificance of household head educational attainment categories and gender and age of child in linear regressions above												
F(5,2407)	2.35	1.23	0.29	1.15	1.45	1.52	0.51	1.28	0.64	0.87	0.84	1.31
Prob>F	0.0385	0.2905	0.9184	0.3340	0.2018	0.1808	0.7659	0.2687	0.6713	0.4992	0.5224	0.2547
Panel D: Test of joint insignificance of household educational attainment dummies, gender of child, age of child, number of siblings of child, household head's age and marital status in linear regressions above												
F(8,2407)	2.81	1.27	0.28	0.94	2.10	1.24	0.51	0.93	2.27	0.99	1.39	1.49
Prob>F	0.0042	0.2531	0.9737	0.4785	0.0323	0.2685	0.8460	0.4908	0.0204	0.4423	0.1971	0.1544

Note: **: P<0.01, *: P<0.05. Standard errors are clustered by household identifier. Administrative register information from Statistics Denmark for the balanced sample of refugee children (described in the footnote to Table 1).

Table A3: Correlation between municipality crime measures and other municipality characteristics for all Danish municipalities over the 1986-1998 period.

	Youth crime conviction rate (%)	Overall crime conviction rate (%)	Reported crimes per capita (%)	Reported violent crimes/ 10,000 inhabitants	Ln(inha bitants)	Relative poverty rate (%)	Immigr ant share (%)	Crime dectection rate (%)	Police officers/ 1000 inhab.	Pupils/ teacher ratio	Mean	StdD
Youth crime conviction rate (%)	1										2.05	0.78
Overall crime conviction rate (%)	0.82	1									0.70	0.24
Reported crimes per capita (%)	0.50	0.64	1								7.14	3.19
Reported violent crimes/10,000	0.43	0.49	0.62	1							17.56	10.14
Ln(inhabitants)	0.33	0.52	0.62	0.35	1						9.40	0.79
Relative poverty rate (%)	0.20	0.23	0.23	0.10	0.12	1					5.87	1.55
Immigrant share (%)	0.44	0.57	0.54	0.41	0.53	0.03	1				2.84	2.39
Crime detection rate (%)	0.02	0.06	0.05	0.19	0.01	0.28	-0.09	1			20.02	4.96
Police officers/1000 inhabitants	0.28	0.33	0.30	0.25	0.18	0.14	0.45	-0.01	1		1.25	0.45
Pupils/teacher ratio	0.27	0.32	0.37	0.26	0.45	-0.07	0.45	-0.09	0.11	1	19.94	1.45
Weekly number of teacher hours/pupil	0.38	0.39	0.37	0.24	0.31	0.01	0.40	-0.09	0.25	0.07	2.39	0.24
N					3,588							

Note: The youth crime conviction rates and the overall crime conviction rates are calculated using the Central Police Register for the age group of 15-25 year old individuals in Denmark and for all residents in Denmark in the period 1986-1998. respectively. The number of reported (violent) crimes is the number of reported (violent) offenses against the penal code from "Statistiske Efterretninger om Social Sikring og Retsvæsen", Statistics Denmark (1986-1998). The source of the number of inhabitants is BEF1A/Statistikbanken/Statistics Denmark. Relative poverty is constructed on the basis of the administrative tax and income registers from Statistics Denmark. The immigrant share is constructed on the basis of the administrative population registers from Statistics Denmark. The information on the crime detection rate comes from "Statistiske Efterretninger om social sikring og retsvæsen", Statistics Denmark (1986-1999). The information on police officers comes from annual police reports (1986-1999). The information on teacher wage hours per pupil comes from "Folkeskolen i de enkelte kommuner", Ministry of Education (1989/90, 1990/91, 1991-92 and 1992/93). The information on pupils/teacher ratio stem from "Folkeskolen i de enkelte kommuner", Ministry of Education (1989/90, 1990/91, 1991/92 and 1992/93) and "Folkeskolen i tal", Ministry of Education (1993/94,1994/95,1995/96,1996/97, 1997/98, 1998/99).

Table A4: Crime categorization. Main categories and main subcategories of crimes in the Central Police Register and our main categories of crimes.

Code/act violated	Main categories and main subcategories of crimes in the Central Police Register	Category	Category description
Penal code	1. All sexual assault convictions	1	Violence
	Rape	1	Violence
	Offense against decency (flasher)	1	Violence
	Sexual offense against children under the age of 12	1	Violence
	Other sexual assault convictions	1	Violence
	2. All violence convictions	1	Violence
	Violence against public authority	1	Violence
	Simple violence	1	Violence
	Threats	1	Violence
	Manslaughter	1	Violence
	Other violence convictions	1	Violence
	3. All offenses against property	2	Property crime
	Document fraud	2	Property crime
	Burglary in bank or shop	2	Property crime
	Shoplifting, etc.	2	Property crime
	Vandalism	2	Property crime
	Fraud	2	Property crime
	Other offenses against property	2	Property crime
	4. Other offenses against the penal code		
	Perjury	4	Other crimes
	Privacy violation and defamation	4	Other crimes
	Negligent manslaughter (road accident)	4	Other crimes
	Sale of narcotics	3	Drug crimes
	Other offenses against the penal code	4	Other crimes
Traffic Act	5. Offenses against the Traffic Act		Excluded
	Drunk driving		Excluded
	Other offenses against the Traffic Act (e.g., speeding)		Excluded
Special Acts	6. All offenses against the Drugs Act	3	Drug crimes
	7. All offenses against the Arms Act	4	Other crimes
	8. All offenses against tax acts and other special acts	4	Other crimes
	Other criminal special laws	4	Other crimes
	Laws concerning gambling and trade	4	Other crimes
	Tax and duty law, etc.	4	Other crimes
	Other offenses against tax acts and other special acts	4	Other crimes

Table A5.A: Variable definitions and primary data sources: Individual characteristics.

Variable	Definition	Primary data source
Criminal conviction in age range a_1-a_2	Dummy for having been convicted (i.e., found guilty) of an offense (except traffic offenses) committed in age range a1-a2 (15-21, 15-17 and 18-21).	Central Police Register, Statistics Denmark (DST).
Criminal conviction of type j in age range a_1-a_2	Dummy for having been convicted (i.e., found guilty) of an offense (except traffic offenses) of type j in age range a1-a2 (15-21, 15-17 and 18-21) (j=violence or sexual assualt, property crime, drugs crime, other crimes).	Central Police Register, DST.
Number of criminal convictions in age range a1-a2	Number of convictions for offenses (except traffic offenses) committed in age range a1-a2 (15-21, 15-17 and 18-21).	Central Police Register, DST.
Number of criminal convictions of type j in age range a1-a2	Number of convictions for offenses (except traffic offenses) committed in age range a1-a2 (15-21, 15-17 and 18-21) (j=violence or sexual assualt, property crime, drugs crime, other crimes).	Central Police Register, DST.
Woman	Dummy for female.	Population register, DST.
Age	Age.	Population register, DST.
Single parent	Dummy for living in a single-parent household.	Population register, DST.
Nuclear family	Dummyfor living in a two-parent household.	Population register, DST.
Number of siblings	Number of persons living in the household after subtraction of the number of parents living in the household and 1 for individual i.	Population register, DST.
Years of education	Number of years of education before immigration, constructed based on an education code of the highest degree attained before immigration.	Survey-based register on immigrants' educational attainment before immigration, DST.
Source country	Dummy for source country.	Population register, DST.
Assignment year	Dummy for first year of receipt of residence permit.	Population register, DST.
Ethnic population	Number of immigrants and descendants of immigrants from the same source country as individual i.	Population register, DST. Authors' calculations based on full population data.

Table A5.B Variable definitions and primary data sources: Area Characteristics.

Variable	Definition	Primary data source
Youth crime conviction rate (%)	Share of individuals aged 15-25 living in municipality convicted of an offense (except traffic offenses) committed in that calendar year.	Central Police Register, DST
Type-specific youth crime convictions rates (%)	Share of individuals aged 15-25 living in municipality convicted of an offense (except traffic offenses) of type j committed in that calendar year (j=violent,property, drugs, other crimes).	Central Police Register, DST
Overall crime conviction rate (%)	Share of individuals living in municipality convicted of an offense (except traffic offenses) committed in that calendar year.	Central Police Register, DST
Type-specific crime convictions rates (%)	Share of individuals living in the municipality convicted of an offense of type j committed in that calendar year (j=violent,property, drugs, other crimes).	Central Police Register, DST
Reported crimes per capita (%)	Number of reported crimes in a given calendar year divided by the number of inhabitants livng in the municipality (or police district) in that year.	"Statistiske Efterretninger om Social Sikring og Retsvæsen", DST (1986-1998).
Reported violent crimes per 10,000 inhabitants	Number of reported violent crimes in a given calendar year divided by the number of inhabitants livng in the municipality (or police district) in that year and multiplied by 10,000.	"Statistiske Efterretninger om Social Sikring og Retsvæsen", DST (1986-1998).
Ln(inhabitants)	Natural logarithm of the number of inhabitants in the municipality.	www.statistikbanken.dk/BEF1A
Relative poverty rate (%)	Share of adults in the municipality who have equivalence-scaled disposable household income <50% of national median equivalence-scaled disposable household income.	Tax and income registers, DST. Authors' calculations based on full population data.
Immigrant share (%)	Number of immigrants and descendants of immigrants living in the municipality divided by the number of inhabitants in the municipality.	Population register, DST. Authors' caluclations based on full population data.
Crime detection rate (%)	Annual number of charges divided by the annual number of reported crimes in the municipality (or police district).	Statistiske Efterretninger om social sikring og retsvæsen, Statistics Denmark (1986-1999).
Police officers per 1,000 inhabitants	Sum of number of detectives and uniformed police officers employed in the police district.	Annual reports from the Police (1986-1999).
Pupils/teacher ratio	Average number of pupils in a normal class in the municipality in a given school year.	"Folkeskolen i de enkelte kommuner", Ministry of Education (1989/90, 1990/91, 1991/92, 1992/93) and "Folkeskolen i tal", Ministry of Education (1993/94, 1994/95, 1995/96, 1996/97, 1997/98, 1998/99)
Weekly number of teacher wage hours per pupil	Weekly number of teacher wage hours per pupil in the municipality in a given school year.	"Folkeskolen i de enkelte kommuner", Ministry of Education (1989/90, 1990/91, 1991/92, 1992/93).

Note: Administrative register information from Statistics Denmark for the balanced sample of refugee children (described in the footnote to Table 1).

Table A6: Effect of a standard deviation increase in municipality crime conviction rates on living in Denmark in all years between age 15 and 21. Full sample of refugee children.

	1	2	3
Youth crime conviction rate	0.002		
	(0.008)		
Youth violent crime conviction rate		0.041	
		(0.058)	
Overall crime conviction rate			0.005
			(0.007)
Controls:			
Gender	Yes	Yes	Yes
Country of origin, year, and age at assignment FE; Family background, size ethnic group DK	Yes	Yes	Yes
N		5,615	

Note: *** p<0.01, ** p<0.05, * p<0.1. Robust standard errors clustered by the municipality of assignment (204 cells) are reported in parentheses. Administrative register information from Statistics Denmark for the full sample of refugee children: Immigrant children from one of the following refugee-sending country: Iraq, Iran, Vietnam, Sri Lanka, Lebanon, Ethiopia, Afghanistan and Somalia, who immigrated before age 15 in the period 1986-1998 and at most one year later than their refugee parent(s) and who turn 21 years old in the period 1986-2006. Family background and municipality of assignment crime measures refer to the year of assignment. There are 5,615 individuals in the full sample of refugee children. The balanced sample of refugee children has 4,425 individuals. Excluded are i) childcren in the full sample of refugee children who have emigrated before age 21 (975 individuals) and ii) children in the full sample of refugee children who live in Denmark at age 21, but are not observed annually in the administrative registers between the age of 15-21 (215 individuals).

Table A7: Summary statistics: Mean (standard deviation) of personal attributes in the year of assignment of refugee children.

	All	Men	Women
Woman	.446 (.497)	0	1
Age	8.59 (3.66)	8.54 (3.68)	8.65 (3.63)
Single parent	.195 (.397)	.193 (.395)	.199 (.399)
Nuclear family	.801 (.399)	.805 (.396)	.797 (.403)
Number of siblings	2.78 (1.86)	2.75 (1.88)	2.83 (1.83)
Educational attainment by age 21:			
Less than 9 years of education	.059 (.236)	.071 (.256)	.046 (.209)
9 years of education	.217 (.412)	.233 (.423)	.197 (.398)
10 years of education	.433 (.496)	.440 (.496)	.426 (.495)
11 years of education	.139 (.346)	.135 (.341)	.146 (.353)
12 or more years of education	.151 (.358)	.122 (.328)	.186 (.389)
Father's educational attainment:			
0-9 years of education	.123 (.328)	.123 (.329)	.122 (.328)
10-12 years of education	.290 (.454)	.297 (.457)	.282 (.450)
More than 12 years of education	.158 (.365)	.164 (371)	.150 (.357)
Unknown	.429 (.495)	.416 (.493)	.445 (.497)
Mother's educational attainment:			
0-9 years of education	.226 (.418)	.227 (.419)	.224 (.417)
10-12 years of education	.319 (.465)	.319 (.466)	.312 (.464)
More than 12 years of education	.113 (.316)	.113 (.317)	.113 (.316)
Unknown	.346 (.476)	.341 (.474)	.351 (.477)
Father's age	32.62 (17.64)	32.98 (17.23)	32.18 (18.14)
Mother's age	33.99 (10.93)	33.63 (11.19)	34.45 (10.58)
Source country:			
Iraq	.145 (.352)	.139 (.346)	.154 (.361)
Iran	.161 (.368)	.165 (.371)	.157 (.364)
Vietnam	.106 (.308)	.107 (.309)	.106 (.308)
Sri Lanka	.090 (.286)	.084 (.278)	.097 (.297)
Lebanon (no citizenship)	.383 (.486)	.387 (.487)	.377 (.485)
Ethiopia	.003 (.054)	.003 (.053)	.003 (.055)
Afghanistan	.036 (.187)	.038 (.191)	.034 (.183)
Somalia	.075 (.263)	.077 (.267)	.072 (.258)
N	4425	2453	1972

Note: Administrative register information from Statistics Denmark for the balanced sample of refugee children (described in the footnote to Table 1).

Table A8. Correlation matrix for number of convictions in age range 15-17 and 18-21.

| | Panel A: Men | | | | | | | |
| | Number of convictions in age range 18-21 | | | | | | | |
	0	1	2	3	4	5 or more	Total	%
Number of convictions in age range 15-17								
0	1328	233	72	30	9	10	1682	68.57
1	221	113	44	15	9	17	419	17.08
2	53	25	18	15	12	26	149	6.07
3	12	12	21	6	10	23	84	3.42
4	5	6	7	7	12	13	50	2.04
5 or more	4	5	4	11	9	36	69	2.81
Total	1623	394	166	84	61	125	2453	
%	66.16	16.06	6.77	3.42	2.49	5.10		100.00
N				2,453				

| | Panel B: Women | | | | | | | |
| | Number of convictions in age range 18-21 | | | | | | | |
	0	1	2	3	4	5 or more	total	%
Number of convictions in age range 15-17								
0	1708	79	17	3	0	1	1808	91.68
1	114	16	4	0	0	0	134	6.80
2	18	3	2	1	0	0	24	1.22
3	1	0	0	1	0	1	3	0.15
4	0	0	0	0	0	0	0	0.00
5 or more	1	0	0	0	0	2	3	0.15
Total	1842	98	23	5	0	4	1972	
%	93.41	4.97	1.17	0.25	0.00	0.20		100.00
N				1,972				

Note: Administrative register information from Statistics Denmark for the balanced sample of refugee children (described in the footnote to Table 1).

Table A9.A: Effect of a standard deviation increase in characteristics of the municipality of assignment on conviction probability and number of convictions in the 15-21 age range. Men.

	1	2	3	4	5	6	7	8	9	10	11	12	13	14
Panel A: Convicted in the 15-21 age range														
Poverty rate (%)	-0.002	0.033												
	(0.009)	(0.033)												
Immigrant share (%)			-0.005	0.052										
			(0.009)	(0.033)										
ln(inhabitants)					-0.001	0.624								
					(0.009)	(0.630)								
Weekly teacher hours per pupil							-0.002	-0.003						
							(0.009)	(0.011)						
Pupils/teacher ratio									-0.005	-0.035*				
									(0.011)	(0.019)				
Crime detection rate (%)											0.006	-0.001		
											(0.011)	(0.014)		
Police officers/1000 inhabitants													0.002	-0.098
													(0.008)	(0.074)
Panel B: Number of convictions in the 15-21 age range														
Poverty rate (%)	0.014	0.067												
	(0.046)	(0.150)												
Immigrant share (%)			0.041	0.089										
			(0.045)	(0.163)										
ln(inhabitants)					0.052	3.536								
					(0.050)	(3.307)								
Weekly teacher hours per pupil							0.098**	-0.002						
							(0.046)	(0.071)						
Pupils/teacher ratio									0.024	-0.102				
									(0.049)	(0.069)				
Crime detection rate (%)											0.048	0.017		
											(0.080)	(0.130)		
Police officers/1000 inhabitants													0.088	-0.696**
													(0.057)	(0.289)
Controls:														
Personal background characteristics	Yes	Yes	Yes	Yes	Yes	Yes	Yes	Yes	Yes	Yes	Yes	Yes	Yes	Yes
Municipality of assignment FE	No	Yes	No	Yes	No	Yes	No	Yes	No	Yes	No	Yes	No	Yes
N								4,425						

Note: ***p<0.01, **p<0.05, *p<0.10. Robust standard errors clustered by the municipality of assignment (204 cells) are reported in parentheses. Administrative register data from Statistics Denmark for the balanced sample of refugee children (described in the footnote to Table 1).

Table A9.B: Effect of a standard deviation increase in characteristics of the municipality of assignment on conviction probability and number of convictions in the 15-21 age range. Men.

	1	2	3	4	5	6	7	8	9	10	11	12	13	14
Panel A: Convicted in the 15-21 age range														
Crime conviction rate (%)	0.023*	0.035*	0.028**	0.049**	0.021*	0.038*	0.020*	0.036*	0.021*	0.041*	0.016	0.034	0.022*	0.043**
	(0.012)	(0.021)	(0.013)	(0.021)	(0.012)	(0.022)	(0.012)	(0.022)	(0.012)	(0.021)	(0.012)	(0.021)	(0.012)	(0.021)
Poverty rate (%)	-0.014	0.024												
	(0.013)	(0.034)												
Immigrant share (%)			-0.021*	0.061										
			(0.012)	(0.037)										
ln(inhabitants)					-0.010	0.669								
					(0.011)	(0.657)								
Weekly teacher hours per pupil							-0.010	-0.006						
							(0.009)	(0.011)						
Pupils/teacher ratio									-0.013	-0.042**				
									(0.012)	(0.020)				
Crime detection rate (%)											0.005	-0.002		
											(0.011)	(0.014)		
Police officers/1000 inhabitants													-0.010	-0.123
													(0.011)	(0.078)
Panel B: Number of convictions in the 15-21 age range														
Crime conviction rate (%)	0.141**	0.140	0.133*	0.171*	0.110*	0.143	0.089	0.128	0.121**	0.161	0.109**	0.137	0.091	0.155
	(0.065)	(0.103)	(0.070)	(0.102)	(0.064)	(0.105)	(0.056)	(0.101)	(0.055)	(0.103)	(0.053)	(0.101)	(0.066)	(0.099)
Poverty rate (%)	-0.059	0.029												
	(0.065)	(0.163)												
Immigrant share (%)			-0.036	0.113										
			(0.067)	(0.176)										
ln(inhabitants)					0.008	3.694								
					(0.063)	(3.434)								
Weekly teacher hours per pupil							0.067	-0.010						
							(0.054)	(0.077)						
Pupils/teacher ratio									-0.025	-0.133*				
									(0.049)	(0.068)				
Crime detection rate (%)											0.038	0.013		
											(0.080)	(0.131)		
Police officers/1000 inhabitants													0.039	-0.789***
													(0.070)	(0.301)
Controls:														
Personal background characteristics	Yes	Yes	Yes	Yes	Yes	Yes	Yes	Yes	Yes	Yes	Yes	Yes	Yes	Yes
Municipality of assignment FE	No	Yes	No	Yes	No	Yes	No	Yes	No	Yes	No	Yes	No	Yes
N								4,425						

Note: *** p<0.01, ** p<0.05, * p<0.10. Robust standard errors clustered by the municipality of assignment (204 cells) are reported in parentheses. Administrative register data from Statistics Denmark for the balanced sample of refugee children (described in the footnote to Table 1).

Table A10: Effect of a standard deviation increase in type-specific youth crime conviction rates in the municipality of assignment in year of assignment on the number of convictions. Men.

	Dependent variable:					
	Number of convictions in age range					
	15-21		15-17		18-21	
	1	2	3	4	5	6
(In %)						
Panel A						
Youth violent crime conviction rate	0.183***	0.179**	0.084***	0.089**	0.099**	0.090*
	(0.066)	(0.079)	(0.031)	(0.036)	(0.041)	(0.054)
Panel B						
Youth property crime conviction rate	0.070	0.090	0.036	0.058	0.034	0.033
	(0.065)	(0.107)	(0.035)	(0.053)	(0.037)	(0.063)
Panel C						
Youth drugs crime conviction rate	-0.075	0.002	-0.048	0.000	-0.027	0.001
	(0.063)	(0.084)	(0.032)	(0.041)	(0.038)	(0.056)
Panel D						
Youth conviction rate of other offences	0.097	0.101	0.050	0.057	0.047	0.044
	(0.069)	(0.085)	(0.031)	(0.039)	(0.043)	(0.055)
Controls:						
As in Specification 4, Table 3	Yes	Yes	Yes	Yes	Yes	Yes
Municipality of assignment FE	No	Yes	No	Yes	No	Yes
N			4,425			

Note: ***: P<0.01, **:P<0.05, *:P<0.10. Robust standard errors clustered by the municipality of assignment (204 cells) are reported in parentheses. Administrative register information from Statistics Denmark for the balanced sample of refugee children (described in the footnote to Table 1). Family background and municipality of assignment characteristics refer to the year of assignment. Mean (standard deviation) of type-specific youth crime conviction rates (of 15-25 year olds) in the municipality of assignment and year of assignment (in percentages) prior to standardization as deviations from the mean relative to the standard deviation: Violence assault: 0.286 (0.123), Property crime: 1.782 (0.528), Drugs offences: 0.301 (0.238) and other offences: 0.342 (0.159).

Table A11: Effect of a standard deviation increase in type-specific youth crime conviction rates in the municipality of assignment in year of assignment on type-specific convictions in the 15-21 age range. Men.

	Dependent variable:							
	Convicted of an offense of type j				Number of convictions of an offense of type j			
	Violent crime and sexual assualt	Property crime	Drugs crime	Other crimes	Violent crime and sexual assualt	Property crime	Drugs crime	Other crimes
	1	2	3	4	5	6	7	8
(In %)								
Panel A								
Youth violent crime conviction rate	0.017**	0.035***	0.015**	0.008	0.034**	0.117***	0.020*	0.012
	(0.008)	(0.011)	(0.006)	(0.009)	(0.015)	(0.043)	(0.011)	(0.012)
Panel B								
Youth property crime conviction rate	0.010	0.011	0.012*	0.004	0.015	0.029	0.008	0.017
	(0.009)	(0.011)	(0.007)	(0.009)	(0.018)	(0.043)	(0.009)	(0.013)
Panel C								
Youth drugs crime conviction rate	0.004	-0.017	-0.005	0.004	-0.015	-0.075*	-0.005	0.019
	(0.010)	(0.012)	(0.006)	(0.008)	(0.021)	(0.040)	(0.011)	(0.012)
Panel D								
Youth crime conviction rate of other offenses	0.020**	0.018	0.001	0.012	0.026	0.037	-0.001	0.035**
	(0.009)	(0.011)	(0.006)	(0.008)	(0.020)	(0.043)	(0.010)	(0.014)
N				4,425				

Note: ***$p<0.01$, **$p<0.05$, *$p<0.10$. Robust standard errors clustered by the municipality of assignment (204 cells) are reported in parentheses. Administrative register information from Statistics Denmark for the balanced sample of refugee children (described in the footnote to Table 1). Controls: As in Specification (4), Table 3. Family background and municipality of assignment characteristics refer to the year of assignment. Mean (standard deviation) of type-specific youth crime conviction rates in the municipality of assignment and year of assignment (in percentages) prior to standardization as deviations from the mean relative to the standard deviation: Violence and sexual assalt: 0.286 (0.123), Property crime: 1.782 (0.528), Drug offenses: 0.301 (0.238) and other offenses: 0.342 (0.159).

Table A12: Effect of a standard deviation increase in different crime measures in the municipality of assignment on the number of convictions. Men.

	Dependent variable:	
	Number of convictions in 15-21 age range	
	1	2
Panel A		
Youth crime conviction rate	0.106*	0.169*
	(0.063)	(0.097)
Panel B		
Youth violent crime conviction rate	0.183***	0.179**
	(0.066)	(0.079)
Panel C		
Number of reported crimes per capita	0.001	-0.152
	(0.078)	(0.118)
Panel D		
Number of reported violent crimes per 10,000 inhabitants	0.094	-0.071
	(0.070)	(0.103)
Panel E		
Youth crime conviction rate	0.113	0.173
	(0.077)	(0.108)
Number of reported crimes per capita	-0.054	-0.177
	(0.088)	(0.124)
Panel F		
Youth violent crime conviction rate	0.176***	0.194**
	(0.067)	(0.078)
Number of reported violent crimes per 10,000 inhabitants	0.024	-0.133
	(0.069)	(0.098)
Panel G		
Youth crime conviction rate	0.216*	0.367**
	(0.128)	(0.160)
Overall crime conviction rate	-0.178	-0.418**
	(0.154)	(0.199)
Panel H		
Youth violent crime conviction rate	0.247**	0.320***
	(0.095)	(0.102)
Overall violent crime conviction rate	-0.086	-0.219*
	(0.087)	(0.112)
Controls:		
As in Specification (4), Table 3	Yes	Yes
Municipality of assignment F.E.	No	Yes
N	4,425	

Note: ***p<0.01, **p<0.05, *p<0.10. Robust standard errors clustered by the municipality of assignment (204 cells) are reported in parentheses. Administrative register information from Statistics Denmark for the balanced sample of refugee children (described in the footnote to Table 1). Youth crime conviction rate: 2.47 (0.70), overall crime conviction rate: 0.95 (0.31), number of reported crimes per capita: 7.25 (3.17), number of reported violent crimes per 10,000 inhabitants: 17.16 (9.63), overall violent crime conviction rate: 0.09 (0.03), youth violent crime conviction rate: 0.29 (0.12).

Table A13: Effect of a standard deviation increase in different youth crime conviction rates on the number of convictions. Men.

					Dependent Variable: Number of convictions in the 15-21 age range					
	1	2	3	4	5	6	7	8	9	10
Youth crime conviction rate										
All	0.106*	0.169*	0.096	0.214**	0.089	0.159	0.103	0.163*	0.090	0.153
	(0.063)	(0.097)	(0.064)	(0.097)	(0.065)	(0.098)	(0.062)	(0.096)	(0.065)	(0.096)
Immigrants and descendants			0.025	-0.127*						
			(0.071)	(0.072)						
Immigrants and descendants from refugee-sending countries					0.099	0.017				
					(0.085)	(0.104)				
Co-nationals							0.105**	0.098**	0.104**	0.096**
							(0.047)	(0.043)	(0.048)	(0.044)
Immigrants and descendants from other refugee-sending countries									-0.043	-0.089
									(0.061)	(0.063)
Controls:										
As in Specification (4), Table 3	Yes	Yes	Yes	Yes	Yes	Yes	Yes	Yes	Yes	Yes
Municipality of assignment F.E.	No	Yes	No	Yes	No	Yes	No	Yes	No	Yes
N					4,425					

Note: ***p<0.01, **p<0.05, *p<0.10. Robust standard errors clustered by the municipality of assignment (204 cells) are reported in parentheses. Administrative register information from Statistics Denmark for the balanced sample of refugee children (described in the footnote to Table 1). Mean (standard deviation) of the different youth crime rates (in %) in the municipality of assignment before standardization as deviations from the mean relative to the standard deviation: Youth crime conviction rate: 2.47 (.70), youth crime conviction rate of immigrants and descendants: 3.86 (2.55), youth crime conviction rate of immigrants and descendants from refugee-sending countries in sample: 4.64 (5.65), youth crime conviction rate of co-nationals: 4.99 (5.65), youth crime conviction rate of immigrants and descendants from other refugee-sending countries: 4.46 (7.36).

Table A14. Initial age structure of sample.

Age at immigration	Year of immigration													N
	1986	1987	1988	1989	1990	1991	1992	1993	1994	1995	1996	1997	1998	
0	1													1
1	92													92
2	73	93												166
3	83	77	50											210
4	75	80	37	61										253
5	74	83	28	55	52									292
6	55	82	43	63	54	57								354
7	52	66	46	50	54	61	52							381
8	41	59	36	55	53	42	48	42						376
9	38	54	23	43	39	47	58	26	27					355
10	42	45	22	42	46	45	45	25	19	20				351
11	43	36	20	38	31	45	59	26	19	24	30			371
12	29	36	22	37	44	45	44	45	18	24	40	22		406
13	28	42	21	28	21	35	53	30	21	15	32	32	54	412
14	20	33	27	37	28	41	47	31	19	25	33	23	41	405
N	746	786	375	509	422	418	406	225	123	108	135	77	95	4425

Note: Administrative register information from Statistics Denmark for the balanced sample of refugee children (described in the footnote to Table 1).

Table A15: Effect of a standard deviation increase in the youth crime conviction rate, by groups of age at assignment. Men.

	Panel 4: Dependent variable: Convicted in age range					
	15-21		15-17		18-21	
	1	2	3	4	5	6
Youth crime conviction rate*assigned before age 6	-0.001	0.024	-0.001	0.013	0.004	0.017
	(0.019)	(0.026)	(0.017)	(0.024)	(0.020)	(0.027)
Youth crime conviction rate*assigned between age 6 and 9	0.014	0.037	-0.005	0.009	0.029	0.038
	(0.026)	(0.033)	(0.021)	(0.026)	(0.020)	(0.026)
Youth crime conviction rate*assigned between age 10 and 14	0.043***	0.057**	0.037**	0.045**	0.031**	0.034
	(0.013)	(0.023)	(0.015)	(0.020)	(0.013)	(0.021)
	Panel B: Dependent Variable: Number of convictions in age range					
	15-21		15-17		18-21	
	1	2	3	4	5	6
Youth crime conviction rate*assigned before age 6	0.081	0.142	0.047	0.100*	0.034	0.042
	(0.078)	(0.104)	(0.041)	(0.052)	(0.055)	(0.075)
Youth crime conviction rate*assigned between age 6 and 9	0.052	0.118	0.008	0.057	0.044	0.061
	(0.092)	(0.121)	(0.050)	(0.066)	(0.056)	(0.070)
Youth crime conviction rate*assigned between age 10 and 14	0.160*	0.214*	0.083***	0.122**	0.077	0.092
	(0.083)	(0.114)	(0.042)	(0.056)	(0.048)	(0.065)
Controls:						
As in Specification (4), Table 3	Yes	Yes	Yes	Yes	Yes	Yes
Municipality of assignment FE	No	Yes	No	Yes	No	Yes
Observations in pooled sample			4,425			

Note: ***p<0.01, **p<0.05, *p<0.10. Robust standard errors clustered by the municipality of assignment (204 cells) are reported in parentheses. Administrative register information from Statistics Denmark for the balanced sample of refugee children (described in the footnote to Table 1). Family background and municipality of assignment characteristics refer to the year of assignment. Mean (standard deviation) of the youth crime conviction rate in the municipality of assignment and year of assignment (in percentages) prior to standardization as deviations from the mean relative to the standard deviation: 2.47 (0.70).